Interracial Relationships
in the 21st Century

Interracial Relationships in the 21st Century

Edited by

Earl Smith
WAKE FOREST UNIVERSITY

Angela J. Hattery
WAKE FOREST UNIVERSITY

CAROLINA ACADEMIC PRESS
Durham, North Carolina

Library of Congress Cataloging-in-Publication Data

Interracial relationships in the 21st century / edited by Earl Smith
and Angela Hattery.
     p. cm.
  Includes bibliographical references and index.
  ISBN 978-1-59460-571-0 (alk. paper)
  1. Race relations. 2. Interracial dating. 3. Interracial marriage.
I. Smith, Earl, 1946- II. Hattery, Angela. III. Title.

  HT1521.I58 2009
  306.84'6--dc22

                                        2009001612

CAROLINA ACADEMIC PRESS
700 Kent Street
Durham, North Carolina 27701
Telephone (919) 489-7486
Fax (919) 493-5668
www.cap-press.com

We dedicate this book to all the individuals and families who are working through the struggles and experiencing the joys associated with love-filled relationships, creating families who cross race and ethnic barriers and defy solidly established norms.

Contents

Acknowledgments

Editing a book has unique and unusual challenges. At the forefront of these is the challenge in identifying the top scholars who write on a specific topic; this is furthered by convincing them that it is worth their time to write a piece that they will then entrust to us, as editors, to care for and shepherd through the review and production process. Though there are always authors that one could include and didn't, we exerted a great deal of effort to identify the key scholars who do a range of research and creative writing about interracial couplings, raising interracial children, interracial intimate partner violence, and navigating identity. We thank the contributors for allowing us to include their research and personal stories in our book, for their patience with us as we journeyed closer to completion, and for their steadfast loyalty and dedication in working on issues of inequalities of race and ethnicity and movements for racial reconciliation. We are grateful for the insight and support of our colleagues at Carolina Academic Press, especially Beth Hall.

List of Contributors

Kellina M. Craig-Henderson, Howard University

Wei Ming Dariotis, San Francisco State University

Angela J. Hattery, Wake Forest University

Tracey A. Laszloffy, Alliant University

Kerry Ann Rockquemore, University of Illinois at Chicago

Earl Smith, Wake Forest University

Amy Steinbugler, Dickinson College

George Yancey, University of North Texas

Interracial Relationships
in the 21st Century

Chapter 1

Introduction

Earl Smith & Angela Hattery

This book, *Interracial Relationships in the 21st Century*, is about interracial love and relationships across what Du Bois (1903) called "the color line" among everyday, ordinary people navigating interracial relationships in a variety of public and private settings.

Because these relationships are mostly private and thus hidden from public view, we know very little about them. What we do know, however, is that people of different races, ethnicities, and even of the same sex get married every day even if they don't stay together. They get married in churches, synagogues, or in Las Vegas at a drive-through wedding chapel. Increasingly, more and more couples—both heterosexual and homosexual—are also cohabitating. Very little attention is being paid to these patterns of coupling unless they involve celebrities like Brad Pitt and Angelina Jolie. Or, as the authors in this book all demonstrate, if it is a couple that "violates" the American racial code: an interracial couple.

As we move deeper into the 21st Century, the United States is becoming increasingly diverse in terms of race/ethnicity as well as the national origin of her population. (See Figure 1-1.)

Along with this increasing diversity comes growing rates of interracial relationships across virtually all lines of demarcation. An obvious outgrowth of this is the rise of children of interracial couples who increasingly desire to be identified as biracial or multiracial. The census, which is often slow to respond to social change, altered several categories in its 2000 tally so that now individuals can choose to identify with more than one race, cohabiting couples can

Figure 1-1: U.S. Population by Race/Ethnicity (Census Categories)

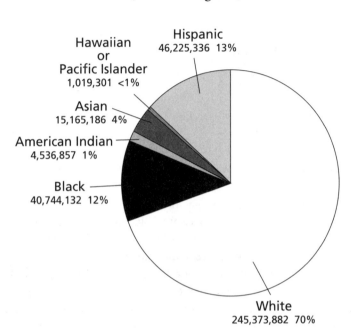

Hawaiian or Pacific Islander
1,019,301 <1%

Hispanic
46,225,336 13%

Asian
15,165,186 4%

American Indian
4,536,857 1%

Black
40,744,132 12%

White
245,373,882 70%

be counted—both heterosexual and homosexual—and, thus, we have better estimates than ever before of the race/ethnic family composition of the U.S. population (Huus 2008).

This book is written in the context of an increasing tolerance for interracial relationships, despite the fact that relatively few people actually enter them. According to Bonilla-Silva (2003), the majority of Americans polled report that they are "OK" with interracial relationships. Yet, census data report that only 5.7 percent of all households in America in 2000 involved interracial marriages and only 12 percent included cohabitating partners of different races. Of further interest is the fact that both race and gender shape the likelihood of entering an interracial marriage. For example, while more than 60 percent of Asian women marry outside of their race, fewer than 5 percent of White men do.

Interracial Marriage among Whites and African Americans

Though the U.S. population is growing increasingly more diverse and we have seen a rise in both the number and percentage of individuals who prefer to identify themselves as multiracial or multicultural, it is imperative that we acknowledge the fact that interracial couplings and "multiracial" children are nothing new. Since the earliest moments of the colonization of what is now the United States by the European conquerors, interracial relationships have existed. For example, Williamson ([1980] 1995), Omi and Winant (1986), and others have noted that intimate relationships among indentured servants, both those from Europe and Africa, were not uncommon. And, it is well documented that both consensual and non-consensual relationships among White men and women of African descent were incredibly common (see Davis 1983; Davis 2006; Omi and Winant 1986; Williamson [1980] 1995). In fact, based on analysis of the 1860 census, Williamson ([1980] 1995) demonstrates that 10% of the African American population at the time was categorized as "mulatto," thus the question of "what to do with the children?" raised by Rockquemore and Laszloffy in their chapter is certainly not a new issue.

Duly noted, this book is not an historical account of interracial relationships, couplings or multiracial children. Furthermore, questions of race/ethnicity and relationships exist in many, if not all, cultures in the world (Cowen 2004). Clearly, the context in the contemporary U.S. was created by a global economy and especially important are both colonization and the slave trade. The U.S. political economy continues to be affected by the trends and politics of immigration (Hattery, Embrick, and Smith 2008). That said, this book is focused on interracial couplings as they exist in the contemporary, 21st-century United States.[1]

---

1. Our companion book looks at the same issues but over time. See Hattery and Smith *Interracial Intimacies: An Examination of Powerful Men and Their Relationships across the Color Line*.

Figure 1-2: Percentage of Married and Cohabiting Americans in Interracial Relationships

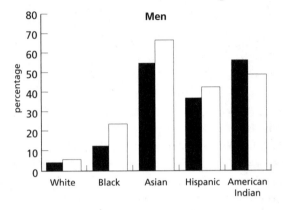

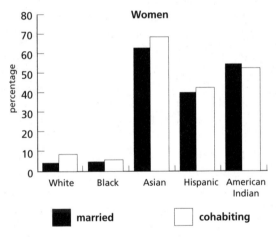

(Qian 2005)

Against the backdrop of an historic moment in the political landscape of the United States, this book was written to be easily accessible as well as academic. For the first time in our more than 200-year history, a major political party nominated a non-white person for the office of President of the United States, Barack Obama. In another first, Obama then went on to become President-elect, winning the election in November 2008. Both throughout the primary season, and increasingly after Obama became the presumptive nominee of the Democratic Party, more and more frequently the news media identified Obama as a biracial man (Carroll 2008).

The son of a White woman from Kansas and an African man from Kenya, Obama is indeed biracial. Yet, this oscillation between identifying him as "African American" or "Black" versus "biracial" illuminates the complex and contested landscape of race, racial identity, and interracial relationships in the United States.[2] During the campaign, many argued that Obama's straddling of the color line made him appeal to a wider range of voters, while others worried that there was still enough resistance among White Americans to prohibit his election to the post of commander-in-chief (Freddoso 2008). On that historic night, November 4, 2008, when Barack Obama won an overwhelming victory to become the 44th president of the United State of America, perhaps some of the concern was put to rest. Yet, in many locations, including on college campuses, racist graffiti immediately began to appear signaling the continued tension around race, racial identity, and interracial relationships in the United States. Thus, this book is both timely and relevant to the American conversation on race.

In order to provide the reader with a broad look at interracial relationships in the contemporary U.S. and beyond, we include chapters that take a scientific approach to interracial relationships, studying them systematically through both interviews and surveys, including a chapter that examines interracial relationships that are plagued by intimate partner violence. We also include a chapter that focuses on raising multiracial children, a topic that is particularly timely and which is brought into unique focus by the presidency of Barack Obama. There are several chapters that are written from the authors' own experiences navigating interracial relationships, both as adults and as the children of such couplings. In one of these chapters, the authors analyze their own experiences with interracial relationships as they are navigated within the context of Christianity.

---

2. The only other figure in America who attracts this kind of overattention as it concerns their racial/ethnic makeup is the professional golfer Tiger Woods. See Smith (2009/2007) for an in-depth discussion.

Given the increasing racial/ethnic diversity in America, we do not limit the book to Black-White relationships (although we do include a chapter on African American men and their relationships with White women), but include chapters on relationships that cross a variety of racial/ethnic and even national boundaries. Though the majority of the chapters focus on heterosexual relationships, we include a chapter that examines interracial relationships among homosexual couples.

One of the strengths and unique features of this book is that as an edited volume it draws on the research and personal experiences of scholars who have distinguished themselves in the study of interracial relationships. This approach also allows for authors to employ different theoretical frameworks for analyzing their data and/or telling their personal stories. As a result, the reader is challenged to think about interracial relationships and all of their nuances from many different angles. Furthermore, we cannot overemphasize the insight into these critical issues that has been brought directly to us via traditional news outlets (e.g., The *New York Times*), and from the newer information streams like podcasts and the blogs. Some of the chapters refer to these sources of information that play a strong role in shaping public opinion on everything from Fair Trade Coffee to ending the death penalty but also including on a regular basis discussions of and debates about interracial relationships.

As we move deeper into the 21st Century and as globalization touches every aspect of our lives—from the products we buy to the intimate relationships we enter—honest, critical forthright discussions of race, racial identity, ethnicity, nationality, religion and interracial relationships will become not only more pertinent but increasingly important (Qian 2005; Qian and Lichter 2007).

The authors of the work collected in this book analyze different aspects of interracial relationships within this context: Americans talk the talk about interraciality but don't necessarily walk the walk when it comes to engaging in interracial couplings and being supportive of these couples and their multi-racial children by offering them the same freedoms as all other Americans, especially Whites.

Though we handle all of the controversies surrounding interracial relationships head-on, we also acknowledge a need for caution; there are still assumptions, stereotypes, and outright fear about these relationships.

These *FEARS* are most often couched in terms of what others might think of the relationship and, just as important, "what about the kids?" In the important paper by Qian and Lichter (2007), we learn the following:

> Recent attitude surveys indicate that Americans are increasingly tolerant of racial intermarriage. In 1997, for example, 67 percent of whites and 83 percent of African Americans approved of such marriages; their support of racial integration in schools, housing, and jobs, however, was even higher. Americans seem comfortable supporting racial integration and equality in public arenas, but they remain comparatively uneasy with interracial sexual intimacy and marriage. Interracial couples often lack the strong social support of families and friends. For example, white and African American adolescents are more likely to introduce same-race partners than different race partners to their families. Qualitative studies also suggest that parents often actively discourage interracial relationships among their children. Parents point to other people's prejudices and express their concerns about the well-being and social acceptance of their mixed-race grandchildren.

While we are reluctant to predict what will happen next, we do know that both immigration and the need for strong, two parent family units are increasing. When we combine this with a tough economy, the color or race, of one's partner becomes less relevant, as long as that partner loves the other, and the other loves them back.

References

Bonilla-Silva, Eduardo. 2003. *Racism without racists: color-blind racism and the persistence of racial inequality in the United States.* Lanham, Md.: Rowman & Littlefield.

Carroll, Jason 2008. "Behind the Scenes: Is Barack Obama black or biracial?" *CNN, http://www.cnn.com/2008/POLITICS/06/09/btsc.obama.race/index.html.*

Cowen, Tyler. 2004. *Creative Destruction: How Globalization Is Changing the World's Cultures.* Princeton, New Jersey: Princeton University Press.

Davis, Angela. 1983. *Women, Race, and Class.* New York: Vintage Books.

Davis, David Brion. 2006. *Inhuman Bondage: The Rise and Fall of Slavery in the New World.* New York: Oxford University Press.

Du Bois, W.E.B. 1903. *Souls of Black Folk,* Edited by A. Herbert. New York: Kraus Thompson Reprint.

Freddoso, David. 2008. *The Case Against Barack Obama.* New York: Regnery Publishing.

Hattery, Angela J., David Embrick, and Earl Smith. 2008. *Globalization and America: Race, Human Rights, and Inequality.* Lanham, Maryland: Rowman & Littlefield Publishers.

Huus, Kari 2008. "Being brown in a city of black and white: Growing up in biracial brothel shaped Detroit woman's view of race." *MSNBC http://www.msnbc.msn.com/id/24726789/page/2/ (Accessed May 28, 2008).*

Omi, Michael and Howard Winant. 1986. *Racial Formation in the United States: From the 1960s to the 1990s.* New York: Routledge and Kegan Paul.

Qian, Zhenchao. 2005. "Breaking the Racial Taboo: Interracial Marriage in America." *Contexts* 4:33–37.

Qian, Zhenchao and Daniel T. Lichter. 2007. "Social Boundaries and Marital Assimilation: Interpreting Trends in Racial and Ethnic Intermarriage." *American Sociological Review* 72:68–94.

Smith, Earl. 2009/2007. *Race, Sport and the American Dream.* Durham, North Carolina: Carolina Academic Press.

Williamson, Joel. [1980] 1995. *New People: Miscegenation and Mulattoes in the United States.* Baton Rouge: Louisiana State University Press.

Chapter 2

African American Attitudes towards Interracial Intimacy: A Review of Existing Research and Findings

Kellina M. Craig-Henderson

Introduction

Today's generation takes for granted that any opposition to interracial relationships is a matter of individual choice. In the 2008 presidential bid for the White House, the biracial Democratic candidate Barack Obama is of African descent. His ascendancy aand election as President of the United States reflects a new era in race relations within the U.S. At no other time has a candidate of African descent enjoyed such wide spread popularity from multi-racial coalitions. As evidence of this, most crowds of his youthful supporters contain placards and vocal supporters who voice the increasingly common expression "Race doesn't matter."

Yet in many ways, race continues to matter. Although relatively scant scholarly attention has focused upon intimate interracial relationships, a great deal of popular attention has increasingly focused on them, suggesting the extent to which race does matter. In general, the tendency among researchers to avoid focusing on these types of arrangements reflects a collective reluctance to deal with two extremely provocative and explosive issues: race and sex. Yet, to the extent that actual rates of interracial relationships continue to increase, discussions about interracial intimacy and the attitudes people have about them are relevant and timely.

Several empirical studies across the social sciences have examined individual attitudes and beliefs about interracial relationships and marriages. Although these studies have varied in terms of their samples, instruments and sophistication, they have generally focused on perceptions of Black-White relationships by White respondents, with those in recent years including samples of African American participants.[1] A few studies, which represent notable exceptions, have focused on African Americans' attitudes towards interracial intimacy. In this chapter, I will review findings from this latter body of work as well as research that includes and compares the responses of African Americans with others.

Importantly, any discussion about contemporary attitudes towards interracial intimacy or the shifts they have undergone should also be accompanied by attention to objective measures of actual rates of participation in interracial intimacy. In 2002, the Census Bureau's Current Population Survey (an annual survey of trends) reported 1,674, 000 interracial marriages which included 395,000 marriages between an African American and a White person. This represents a steady increase over rates recorded in each of the preceding censuses depicted below (1960–to present). (See Figure 2-1.)

What accounts for these changes?

---

1. Throughout this chapter which focuses on African American attitudes I will use the terms "African American" and "Black" interchangeably. Although it is acknowledged that in certain forums the words may differ from one another (e.g., Black people born in England and immigrated to the U.S. may not opt to adopt this moniker), within the current discussion the terms are assumed synonymous unless otherwise stated.

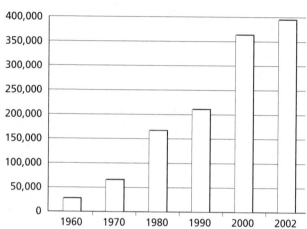

Figure 2-1: Trends in Black-White Marriages
in the United States (1960–2002)

African American Attitudes towards Interracial Intimacy

Results of a 1997 Gallup poll provide evidence of Americans' generally increasingly tolerant attitudes towards interracial marriages. Touted as "one of the most substantial race-related changes ever noted in a Gallup poll," a numerical majority of Black and White Americans expressed acceptance of interracial marriage. According to one article describing these data (Astor, 1997), whereas only 25 percent of Whites approved of interracial marriage in 1972, 61 percent noted their approval in 1997. Blacks also evidenced a change though overall their acceptance of interracial marriage has always been higher than that of Whites, 61 percent noted their approval in 1972, and this increased to 77 percent in 1997. More than anything else, these findings show that acceptance for interracial marriages has generally increased.

Focusing on African American Attitudes

Although it is certainly instructive to review findings from research employing the racial comparative approach, it is important to study African American attitudes as they occur and are expressed in their own context. Much of the research on attitudes that exists across areas has focused largely on the responses of Whites. When people of color have been included it is for the purpose of providing a comparison to Whites. That is, the importance and relevance of their responses is generally based upon the extent to which their responses differ or resemble those of Whites. For the most part, and this extends well beyond research on attitudes, the behavior and responses of Whites are taken as the default against which all others are compared (Asante, 1987; Azibo, 1992).

This is problematic for several reasons, not the least of which is that White respondents are no more "normative" than any other racial group (Azibo, 1992). Second, this kind of comparative racial approach tends to ignore the diversity that exists within the larger grouping of African Americans. For example, there are likely to be differences associated with gender and socioeconomic status among African Americans (Shelton, 2000). A third problem with this kind of approach is that it fails to adequately address the specific experiences of African Americans by focusing on them. Studying the attitudes of African Americans as they exist apart from comparison to Whites or others is informative in its own right. This approach, known as the "emic" approach (Triandis & Marin, 1983), involves an attempt to understand African American attitudes towards interracial relationships based only on data obtained from a sample of African Americans.

Research on African Americans' Attitudes toward Interracial Intimacy

A recent qualitative study focused solely on the experiences of African American men in interracial relationships (Craig-Henderson, 2006). That study involved in-depth analysis of the interview responses of a small but diverse sample of Black men who are currently or were recently involved in interracial relationships. Among other things, the interviews assessed the men's attitudes towards race relations in general and interracial relationships in particular.

Findings from that study provide another way of looking at interracial relationships and people's attitudes about them (Craig-Henderson, 2006). Not surprisingly, most of the respondents included in that study expressed attitudes reflecting personal acceptance and support of interracial relationships. At the same time, however, a number of the men interviewed expressed reservations about race relations in general and their attitudes in some cases revealed less than positive attitudes about members of other racial groups; even the groups in which their partners were members.

It is also important to note that within a subgroup of the respondents included in that study there were those who disclosed having had negative attitudes towards interracial intimacy (particularly involving Blacks) before becoming personally involved in an intimate interracial relationship. For these men, their behavior altered their subsequent attitudes to interracial intimacy.

In much the same way that earlier sociological approaches viewed rates of interracial marriages as a barometer for the quality of race relations (e.g., Merton, 1941), Mwamwenda (1998) focused on expressed attitudes toward interracial marriage among Blacks in South Africa. In a sample of college students studying psychology, the researcher obtained responses to demographic items and questions reflecting students' and parents' attitudes towards marriage to a White person. Results revealed that both male and female Black university students indicated a preference for marrying a Black person, and reported that their parents would disapprove of an interracial marriage to a White person.

In another study, researchers Jacobson and Johnson (2000) examined the correlates of support for interracial marriage among African Americans by utilizing New York Times poll data from 2000. This study involved the secondary analysis of data, and the findings can be particularly instructive given the unusually large sample (n = 934) of African Americans included in this nationally representative sample. The researchers were interested in associations between a number of variables including education, gender, age, income, geographic region, metropolitan status, and — of greatest interest — interracial friendships and African Americans' expressed attitudes toward interracial marriage.

Findings from their analyses indicate that friendship, defined by respondents' indication of the number of friends they have of a different race and the extent of socializing they've done with someone of a different race in the past month, is a critical variable affecting African Americans' expressed approval of interracial marriage. Respondents' sex and metropolitan status (populated by more or less than 500,000) also demonstrated significant effects. According to the authors, "demographic and structural factors provide opportunities for interracial friendships to develop, which in turn increase the approval of interracial marriage" (Jacobson and Johnson 2000, 580).

In a more recent investigation, Ross (2004) compared college students' perceptions of interracial couples to their perceptions of same-race couples with a focus on the impact of the student's race, age, gender and educational level. The study included 153 students, a third of them African Americans, and involved the completion of the Korolewicz Interracial Dating Preference questionnaire (K-IDPQ). The K-IDPQ is a self-reported questionnaire that consists of twelve scenarios each of which is followed by five questions for respondents to complete.

Overall, and consistent with the researcher's primary and somewhat simplistic prediction, results suggest that participants were more favorable towards same race than different race couples. Additionally, findings from this study also appear to reflect a difference between African American and White participants. Among males and females, African Americans responded more favorably to the interracial scenarios than did White participants. As Ross (2004) notes, this finding is consistent with research reported by a host of other researchers including Mills, Daly, Longmire and Kilbride (1995), Knox, Zusman, Buffington, & Hemphill (2000) and Lee, Campbell and Miller (1991).

The Knox, Zusman, Buffington, & Hemphill (2000) paper reported results of a survey of 620 college students. Although the sample included only a small number of African Americans relative to Whites, it was possible to conclude from the results that African Americans were twice as likely as Whites (83 percent v. 43 percent) to indicate that they were open to the prospect of being in an interracial relationship. Admittedly, there were several shortcomings to this study. However, results provide additional support for the oft-observed finding of greater acceptance of interracial relationships among African Americans.

Given that family of origin likely influences the attitudes that young adults have (Childs, 2002), some researchers have examined the relationship between perceptions of family acceptance and attitudes toward interracial relationships. Mills, Daly, Longmire, and Kilbride (1995) proposed that people reporting more favorable attitudes towards interracial relationships would also report greater family acceptance of interracial relationships. In addition, these researchers expected to find that among respondents, African Americans would express more favorable attitudes towards interracial relationships than would Whites.

In their study (Mills, Doly, et. al. 1995), 142 undergraduate college students responded to a questionnaire developed by the researchers to measure the degree of acceptance of interracial friendships and relationships as well as perceptions of family acceptance. Findings from the study were limited and no effects were found for the impact of the degree of family acceptance on attitudes towards interracial relationships. Instead, participants overwhelmingly acknowledged that race was influential in determining friendships and relationships. Perhaps most interesting, they found that African Americans not only reported more favorable attitudes towards interracial relationships but they also reported having more interracial friendships than did Whites.

The earliest Gallup poll to include African Americans' attitudes toward interracial marriage was conducted in 1968. Results of that early poll revealed that even as far back as 40 years ago, a majority of African Americans have consistently approved of marriages between Blacks and Whites. In the 1968 poll, 56 percent of Blacks said they approved of Black-White unions. This percentage has risen steadily throughout the 1970s the 1980s and early 1990s. By 1997, three in four Blacks approved of interracial marriages, and since 2003, more than 80 percent have approved.

That African Americans and Whites would approach and respond to interracial relationships quite differently is not surprising when one considers the peculiar history of "race" in the United States in conjunction with the system of slavery that characterized relations between Blacks and Whites for more than 400 years (Novkov, 2002). Early on in this history, attention to and discussions about race evolved out of attempts to justify the subjugation of enslaved Africans. The legacy of such historical realities has been a continuing tension in Black-White relations, racial disparities in socioeconomic status, and differences in rates of and favorability toward intimate interracial relationships, among other things (Tucker & Mitchell-Kernan, 1990).

In today's society, a major change in dating and intimate relationships is that they are increasingly more likely to develop through the use of internet dating sites. Today, people "meet" and connect with one another for friendship, love and intimacy on-line. Consequently, the internet can provide a viable means for studying attitudes towards interracial intimacy. A study by Wilson, McIntosh and Insana (2007) implemented this approach in order to learn more about the factors associated with African Americans' dating preferences. The researchers obtained 200 profiles from an equal number of Black men and women available at the Match.com internet matchmaking site.

The profiles were coded according to fourteen demographic variables as well as six variables related to willingness to date interracially. Findings from this study revealed that being young, male, attractive (determined by two independent raters), a smoker, and wanting children were all related to African Americans' willingness to be involved in interracial relationships. These effects were consistent regardless of the specific race they expressed a willingness to date. Specifically, results revealed that younger people were more willing to date interracially than older people; men were significantly more willing to do so than were women; the more attractive the person the more likely they were to express a willingness for dating Whites, Asians or Hispanics; those wanting children were more likely to express a willingness to date Asians and Whites; and the smokers were more willing to date Whites and Hispanics. While the researchers acknowledged the difficulty in explaining some of these findings (e.g., what does smoking have to do with openness to dating interracially?), they highlighted the apparent gender difference in expressed willingness to date someone of another race.

This race difference is consistent with other studies though there are at least two published exceptions to the trend indicating greater favorability toward interracial relationships among African Americans. These exceptions highlight gender differences across race. In a 1991 article, Paset and Taylor studied 50 African American and White college women in order to determine their attitudes towards interracial marriage. In general, findings from their study revealed that White women had a more favorable attitude than Black women. The authors concluded that contemporary differences in availability of mates makes the prospect of interracial marriage appear threatening for Black women in a way that is not the case for White women.[2]

As further support for this conclusion, much has been said across a wide array of forums about the disparity in the number of eligible African American men and women available for dating and marriage. As a result of the dire state of affairs in which Black men exist, most reports note that Black women outnumber Black men. Consider that African American men are incarcerated at proportionally greater rates than Whites (Shelden, Brown, Listwan, 2004),

---

2. Another study by Todd, McKinney, Harris, Chadderton, and Small (1992) found similar results. Black women were found to be the least approving group in the study with almost half of them expressed disapproval with interracial dating and marriage.

their life expectancies are lower and health risks greater (Hoyert, Heron, Murphy, & Kung, 2006), and far fewer of them are college educated and employed in professional settings (Madhubuti, 1990). When these harsh realities are viewed in conjunction with the fact that they are more likely than Black women to be in interracial heterosexual relationships (Kalmijn, 1993, Qian, 1997), it is entirely reasonable for Black women to view at least part of the new trends toward interracial marriage as threatening (Childs, 2005; Craig-Henderson, 2006, 2008). Many African American women see Black men as being largely unavailable and the prospects of being in an intimate relationship with them as unlikely (Craig-Henderson, 2008).

Variation within Race

The research literatures have often treated African Americans as a monolithic group, which they are not. Instead, within the racial group of people who identify as "Black" there are substantial ethnic, cultural, and regional differences. Rarely has research on attitudes towards interracial relationships taken account of these differences, though a few exceptions do exist.

One such exception is a study focusing on rates of intermarriage across America's diverse Black populations. Researchers Batson, Qian, and Lichter (2006) found that rates of interracial marriage with Whites differed by subgroup, gender, and educational attainment. In that paper, data from the 2000 census were used to identify differences in rates of interracial marriage among Black subgroups. Although the study did not focus on attitudes, it is possible to infer something about attitudes from the reports of behavior of the subgroups included in the Census given that the behavior in question was marriage. By highlighting emerging patterns of cohabitation and marriage with Whites among the Black subgroups, these researchers identified several differences likely to be reflected in the attitudes among the different subgroups.

First, the researchers noted that despite higher educational attainment, the immigrant subgroups (including West Indians and

Africans) were less likely to form marital and cohabitating unions with Whites than were African Americans (i.e., native born Blacks). This suggests more positive attitudes toward interracial relationships among those Blacks born in the U.S. than among those originally born elsewhere. On the other hand, the data also reveal that native born Blacks are still more likely to marry other Blacks than they are to marry Whites. With respect to this finding, the researchers caution against attempts to place too much emphasis on this trend given that *intramarriage* between African Americans and Black immigrants is surprisingly low. Lastly, the finding that males from all Black subgroups are more likely than females to be in interracial unions is worth noting. It demonstrates the existence of a gender difference in attitudes among the broader category of "Blacks." Though notable, this observed gender difference has been observed in other research (e.g., in a study I conducted described below and also in the Wilson, McIntosh, and Insana, 2007 paper described above) and serves as a basis for anecdotal contemporary accounts about interracial relationships and African American men and women. I turn now to a study conducted in the Fall of 2007, with a colleague at a historically Black university located in the Southeastern region of the U.S.

Illustration: The HBCU Study

In this project, undergraduate business school majors volunteered to participate in "a study on social attitudes." The design of the study involved the systematic variation of the racial status of the male and female in a Black/White heterosexual couple. The design also varied whether the couple was of high or low socioeconomic status (SES). Each of 58 advanced college students read a short vignette and subsequently responded to a number of Likert-items with responses that ranged from *1* = "strongly agree" to *9* = "strongly disagree." In addition to the Likert questionnaire, which served as the primary dependent variable, respondents also answered a number of demographic items assessing gender, age, region of origin, and racial and marital status. Each of the participants read and responded to a short vignette about a heterosexual couple who in half of all cases included a Black man and a White woman, and in other half the characters were reversed; a Black woman and White man.

In addition to the impact of the racial status of the members of the interracial couple, I was also interested in learning about the extent to which African American attitudes towards interracial couples are influenced by the perceptions of the relative status of the couple. Whether the members of the couple in the vignette were described as professionals employed as attorneys or among the chronically unemployed was systematically varied so that half of all participants read a vignette about an unemployed couple, and half read a vignette about a couple of attorneys.

Among the statistically significant findings worth noting, participants made judgments about the couples as a function of the interracial status of the couple, though these effects were limited to a small number of specific items included on the questionnaire. Whether the heterosexual couple depicted in the vignette included an African American man or woman, and a White man or woman who were attorneys or chronically unemployed impacted judgments about the "difficulties they'd face in the future" ($p < .05$), and "there being too many similar types of couples" ($p < .05$).

Participants indicated that the BM/WW unemployed couple faced the most difficult future together ($M = 4.00$), and this was followed by the BM/WW professional ($M = 3.29$), the BW/WM unemployed ($M = 2.93$), and the BW/WM professional ($M = 2.67$) couples. Participants most strongly disagreed with the statement that "there are too many couples like this" in response to the BW/WM professional ($M = 7.27$) couple; the lowest mean score was for BM/WW professional ($M = 6.07$) couples. Its important to note that despite this variance, all the means were close to the end of the scale indicating strong disagreement. This suggests that participants generally did not perceive there to be too many of any of the types of interracial couples depicted.

Findings from this study reflect the different attitudes African American participants have about interracial Black/White couples. These differences in attitudes are associated with which member of the couple was Black (or White) and whether the couple was perceived to be high in socio-economic status or low. Generally speaking, the participants in this study judged the Black/White interracial couple with the African American man and White woman to be most fraught with difficulty, and although this effect was strongest for the unemployed couple it was also the case for the professionally employed BM/WW couple. In contrast, the interracial couple with the African American woman and White man was perceived to face relatively fewer difficulties in the future.

In a similar vein, participants also distinguished the BM/WW couples from the BW/WM couples in terms of the degree to which they disagreed with the statement that there are too many interracial couples like this. Again, results were primarily associated with whether the man or the woman in the couple was Black (or White). Whereas participants most strongly disagreed that there were too many BW/WM couples, they expressed relatively less disagreement with this statement when applied to BM/WW couples. There was also an interesting finding that emerged as a result of the gender of the participants. Results revealed that more male participants ($M = 3.28$) agreed with the statement "more people should date outside of their race" than did female participants ($M = 2.70$, $p < .05$).

Although a number of participants indicated having non-native ethnic status (i.e., there were six indicating they were born outside of the U.S.), the overall sample size and numbers of those who were not born in the U.S. precluded analysis of participant responses as a function of their nationality. Another important limitation of this study was the extent to which it, like much of the work in this area, ignored differences among the various Black populations (e.g., West Indians, Africans, and African Americans). As noted above, the majority of research on race relations has treated African Americans as a monolithic group.

Concluding Comments

Attitudes towards interracial intimacy are very much a product of the cultural zeitgeist. There have been considerable societal changes that have impacted intergroup and interracial relationships in the U.S. As the quality and regularity of interracial friendships changes, so too does the likelihood that intimate interracial relationships will form. As discussed above, most public opinion polls reveal a decline in White racial prejudice (among Whites), and greater acceptance of social interaction with members of other races. One consequence of this attenuation in racial animus has been an increase in the numbers of African Americans in marriages with Whites; an increase that is reflected in data compiled by the U.S. Census Bureau.

In addition to the increased rates of interracial friendships that are associated with changes in race related attitudes, there are also structural changes that occur. Over the past several decades, neighborhoods have undergone significant changes. These changes have reflected the increased movements of African Americans and other minorities into formerly all White enclaves. Although this process is by no means linearly predictive, the fact that it is underway underscores the role of yet another correlate to increases in rates of interracial intimacy. As neighborhoods become increasingly racially and ethnically diverse, there are more opportunities to meet people and develop friendships and intimate relationships across racial lines.

More African Americans are likely to be in intimate interracial relationships with Whites today than was the case as recently as twenty years ago. What are both determinants and causes of this state of affairs are the attitudes African American have towards interracial intimacy. Although it is true that African Americans have always expressed more favorable attitudes towards interracial intimacy than Whites, the overall level of support expressed has increased over the last few decades, shifting towards even greater acceptance. These relatively positive attitudes lead to greater numbers of African Americans involved in interracial intimacy, and in turn this increase in rates of involvement leads to more positive attitudes among African Americans towards these types of interracial relationships. At the same time, given the different objective conditions that characterize the experiences African American men and women, there are likely to be gender differences apparent in attitudes towards interracial intimacy.

References

Astor, C. 1997 — August. Gallup poll: Progress in Black/White relations, but race is still an issue. *U.S. Society & Values, USIA Electronic Journal 2*: on-line.

Azibo, D.A.Y. 1992. Understanding the proper and improper usage of the comparative research framework. In *African American Psychology*, eds. A.K. Burlew, W. C. Banks, H.P. McAdoo and D.A. Azibo. 18–27. Newbury Park, CA: Sage Publications.

Childs, E.C. 2002. Families on the color-line: patrolling borders and crossing boundaries. *Race and Society* 5(2): 139–161.

Childs, E.C. 2005. Looking behind the stereotypes of the "angry Black woman." *Gender & Society*, 19, 544–561.

Craig-Henderson, K.M. 2006. *Black men in interracial relationships. What's love got to do with it?* Piscataway, NJ; Transaction Publishers, Inc.

Craig-Henderson, K.M. 2008. *Black Women and Interracial Intimacy. Manuscript in preparation.*

Hoyert, D.L., M. Heron, S.L. Murphy and H.C. Kung. January 19, 2006. *Deaths: Final Data for 2003.* Division of Vital Statistics, National Center for Health Statistics. Hyattsville, MD: U.S. Department of Health and Human Services.

Jacobson, C.K. and B.R. Johnson. 2006. Interracial friendship and African American attitudes about interracial marriage. *Journal of Black Studies* 36: 570–584.

Kalmijn, M. 1993. Trends in Black/White Intermarriage. *Social Forces* 72: 119–146.

Knox, D., M.E. Zusman, C. Buffington and G. Hemphill. 2000. Interracial dating attitudes among college students. *College Student Journal* 34 (1): 69–76.

Madhubuti, H. 1990. *Black men: Obsolete, single, dangerous?* Chicago: Third World Press.

Merton, R. 1941. Intermarriage and the social structure: Fact and theory. *Psychiatry* 4: 361–374.

Mills, J.K., J. Daly, A. Longmore and G. Kilbride. 1995. A note on family acceptance involving interracial friendships and romantic relationships. *The Journal of Psychology* 129: 349–351.

Mwamwenda.1998. African university students' responses to questions on interracial marriage. *Psychological Reports* 83: 658.

Novkov, J. 2002 — Summer. Racial Constructions: the Legal Regulation of Miscegenation in Alabama, 1890–1934. *Law and History Review* 20: 225–277.

Paset, P.S. and R.D. Taylor, R.D. 1991. Black and White women's attitudes toward interracial marriage. *Psychological Reports* 69: 753–754.

Qian, Z. 1997. Breaking the racial barriers: Variations in intermarriage between 1980–1990. *Demography* 34: 263–276.

Ross, W. 2004–05. The perceptions of college students about interracial relationships. *National Forum of Applied Educational Research Journal-Electronic,* 17E: 1–16.

Shelden, R.G., W.B. Brown and S.J. Listwan. 2004. The new American apartheid: The incarceration of African Americans. In *For the Common Good*, eds. R. Miller & S. Browning. Durham, NC: Carolina Academic Press.

Shelton, N. 2000. A reconceptualization of how we study issues of racial prejudice. *Personality and Social psychology Review* 4: 374–390.

Todd, J., J.L. McKinney, R. Harris, R. Chadderton and L. Small. 1992. Attitudes toward interracial dating: Effects of age, sex, and race. *Journal of Multicultural Counseling and Development* 20: 202–208.

Triandis, H. C., and G. Marin. 1983. Etic plus emic versus pseudoetic. A test of a basic assumption of contemporary cross-cultural psychology. *Journal of Cross-Cultural Psychology* 14: 489–500.

Tucker, M.B. and C. Mitchell-Kernan. 1990. New trends in Black American Interracial marriage: The Social Structural Context. *Journal of Marriage and the Family* 52: 209–218.

Wilson, S., B., W.D. McIntosh, W.D. and S.P. Insana. 2007. Dating across race. An examination of African American internet personal advertisements. *Journal of Black Studies* 37: 964–982.

Chapter 3

Hapa: An Episodic Memoir

Wei Ming Dariotis

Introduction

I have been struggling for several years with this apparently un-resolvable issue: what to do about "Hapa?" I finally decided I had to start writing about it; I had to start engaging the dialogue. The positionality of mixed race and mixed heritage Asian Americans became more solidly located within Asian American communities at least partially through the naming of them/us as a coherent, iden-tifiable group through the use of the term "Hapa." "Asian American" itself is a term of collective identity that grew out of a political movement—before 1968, one was "Oriental" or Japanese, Chinese, Filipino, or Korean. "Asian American" as a term provides a space in which these disparate ethnic communities can come together, but it also creates it's own sense of identity—what Yen Le Espiritu calls "Asian American pan-ethnicity."[1] As opposed to eth-nic-specific terms like the Filipino "mestizo" or the Japanese "haafu," "Hapa" is a word that specifically situates mixed Asian Americans within this pan-ethnic Asian American community.[2] "Hapa" also provides the important function of giving mixed Asian Americans

---

1. Yen Le Espiritu. *Asian American Panethnicity: Bridging Institutions and Identities.* (Philadelphia: Temple University Press, 1992)

2. My thanks to UC Davis student Ben Jose for helping me articulate this idea.

a safe space. Growing controversies over the use of the Native Hawaiian word "hapa" to identify mixed race Asian Americans could possibly destabilize this unifying identity — or could provide an interesting opportunity to push out the boundaries we may have drawn around ourselves in the process of coming together.

Hapa: Community and Family

I am a queer (bi), "mixed race" Asian American woman — or, in the words of a participant in the research of Beverly Yuen Thompson, a "bi-bi girl."[3] My name is my symbolic passport to both my Asian American and my "mixed race" identities: Wei Ming Dariotis — Chinese and Greek, right up front.[4] My mother told me she chose my Chinese name to balance the Greek, and to give herself the satisfaction of naming her own daughter the way she wished she had been named — with love and care. Names are not to be taken lightly, she told me. My name, Wei Ming, was something she determined would be special. "Wei" contains the characters "book" and "heart" and she translates it to mean both "heart and book knowledge" — that is, "be both wise and understanding." The message of my name is: always "know your heart," she tells me. "Ming" combines the characters for "sun" and "moon," which my mother translates as "shining brilliance." My mother told me that "Wei Ming" was a name I should love calling myself and that I should try to grow into. My mother told me she thought about a child who is told every day that she is stupid — eventually, she may come to believe this about herself. My mother wanted me to believe what my name says about me, and through this she taught me that names are extremely important. They are not just randomly assigned la-

---

3. Beverly Yuen Thompson, "The Politics of Bisexual/Biracial Identity: a Study of Bisexual and Mixed Race Women of Asian/Pacific Islander Descent" (Reno: That Damn Book! and Money to Authors Ink. Publishing, 1999) 31.

bels or markers; rather, names also have the power to shape meaning, identity, and even to create communities.

The queer Vietnamese American poet Truong Tran told me that when he was a young boy his Tolkiensian "ring of power" was the English word "fuck." This word made him American; it was like a secret language, something his parents didn't speak, a word he could claim as his own. He used it gleefully, like Bilbo used the ring, to set himself above where he had been as a disenfranchised, alienated immigrant child.

My ring of power was also a word, the word "Hapa." I first learned this word in 1992, when I was 23 years old. I was a second-year English Literature doctoral student at UC Santa Barbara, and I was enrolled in the course, "The World of Amerasians," taught by Teresa K. Williams.[4] When I learned the word "Hapa" I felt as though a whole new world had opened up to me. Before this, when anybody asked me, "What are you?" I had to answer, "Chinese, Greek, Swedish, English, Scottish, German, Pennsylvania Dutch." This was a list of my ancestry. It is my heritage. However, this list is not my identity. Heritage does not equal identity. To paraphrase the title of the book on Asian Americans of mixed heritage edited by Teresa K. Williams and Cynthia Nakashima, my identity is something more than the *sum of my parts*. "Hapa" gave me such an identity. With the word "Hapa" I had a sense of given community for the first time in my life. The word "Hapa" made me something more than just a "half Chinese" or a "fake Filipino." The word "Hapa" allowed me to be a fully recognized member of the pan-ethnic Asian American community because "Hapas" came to be recognized as a legitimate Asian American group. For example, I was invited to give reports at Asian American Department meetings from the "Hapa unit" — in parallel to the "Japanese American unit" and the "Korean American unit." The word "Hapa" allowed me to com-

---

4. This class is described in detail in William's 1996 essay, "Being Different Together in the University Classroom: Multiracial Identity as Transgressive Education," *In the Multiracial Experience: Racial Borders as the New Frontier*, ed. M. P. P. Root. Thousand Oaks, CA: Sage.

fortably identify as Asian American for the first time in my life because *it was understood to be* an Asian American-focused term — it
didn't just mean "mixed" — it specifically signified "mixed Asian or
Pacific Islander."

War Baby | Love Child (Ang 2001)[5]

Being asked, daily, "What are you?" I was made aware at an early
age that the people who asked me that question wanted to know
something that went beyond my personal identity. They wanted to

---

5 The first version of this essay, published on the Mixed Heritage Center website and, in a different form, as part of the online arm of the Hyphen Magazine Hybrid Issue, is titled, "Hapa: The Word of Power." The
talks have included one at Berkeley in 2003 (panel), another presented
Fall 2007 at Occidental College (with thanks to Lauren Moffett and Julie
Klushnik); "A Name We Can All Love Calling Ourselves" as the Keynote
speech of the Berkeley API Issues Conference, Spring 2008 (with thanks
to student organizer Brian Lau); and the current essay, presented as a part
of Mixed Heritage Week at UC Davis, 5/8/08, organized by the Cross Cultural Center (for which I would like to thank to Dominique Littlejohn and
Center Director Steven Baissa).

My thanks to the students of Occidental College, San Francisco State
University (especially AAS 550: Asian Americans of Mixed Heritage), UC
Davis (ASA 120, Spring 2000 and attendees of "To Be Hapa or Not To Be
Hapa," May 8, 2008), and UC Berkeley; the former members, staff and
Board of Hapa Issues Forum (especially Andrew Bushaw, Anthony Yuen,
Claire Light, Eric Hamako, April Elkjer, and Sheila Chung); the staff and
board of iPride (especially Tarah Fleming, Jilchristina Vest, Andrew Jo-
livette, Jacqueline Miller, and FUSION Summer Camp founder, Joemy
Ito-Gates); Truong Tran; my teacher, Teresa Williams-Leon; Cynthia
Nakashima; Paul Spickard; Laura Kina; Farzana Nayani; Camilla Fojas;
Marianne Maruyama Halpin; Kip Fulbeck; Marlon Hom; Malcolm Col-
lier; Mohammad Salama; Stuart Gaffney; Lori Kay; Kent Ono; Jennifer
Chan; Sachiko Reed; Ayumi Nagase; Aaron Kitashima; Danise Olague; the
many students who have attended my talks and workshops on this topic;
and to Native Hawaiian hapas, all of whom have contributed to the on-
going dialogue that has lead me to write this essay or have acted as sounding boards for these ideas.

know something about my parents, and they were curious because there was something about us as a family; and me as an individual, that was *not normal*. If I answered, "Chinese, Greek, Swedish, Scottish, English, German, and Pennsylvania Dutch," as I usually did, all in one breath, I would then be interrogated regarding which one of my parents is Chinese. Most people assume, correctly, that my mother is Chinese. But why would they assume this, and why would they need to know that, if they really just wanted to know what I am? (Note: The question is not "Who Are You?" it is always, always, always, "What Are You?")

The answer is simple: The Question, "What Are You?" is not really about my individual identity; it is really a question about race and about gender. It is about power: who has it, personally and institutionally, and how it is used in the world. And, ultimately, how creatures like me upset the balance of power by messing up the lines of power. In the process of photographing subjects for his book, *Part Asian, 100% Hapa*, Kip Fulbeck asked participants to write down their answers to the question, "What Are You?" Their answers are reproduced as scrawled in their own hand writing. I was photographed twice for Fulbeck's book, the second time was at someone's apartment in San Francisco, and with me were about 40 other mixed heritage Asian Americans—self-identified Hapas—some of whom I knew but many I was just meeting for the first time. Fulbeck mentioned that he envisioned these gatherings—organized by email blasts—as participating in the construction of "Hapa community." The first time I was photographed the situation was even more consciously a construction of "Hapa community;" during the 2002 Hapa Issues Forum 10th Anniversary Conference, in 2002, which I chaired, Fulbeck set up his photo booth in a private area and invited the 300 attendees to be photographed. I remember in both circumstances being dissatisfied with my answer, and being troubled by the question. "Where did your parents meet?" is most often the follow up to the "What Are You?" question. By those less tactful, but perhaps more honest, this would be phrased, "Was your father in the military?" In other words (and though I've never, ever been asked this, I've often wished I would be, just to see how I might answer): "Are you a War Baby or a Love Child?"

How have I made this leap? I was born in 1969, just two years after the historic Supreme Court decision, *Loving V. Virginia* that struck down the remaining anti-miscegenation laws in 17 states. 1969 was also the height of the escalation of U.S. involvement in Vietnam, and it was at the crux of the Civil Rights and anti-war movements.

The two historical factors that have had the largest impact on the number of Asian and Pacific Americans of mixed heritage are war (and his attendants: colonialism and imperialism) and the Civil Rights movement. Arguably, until recently, war, or at least imperialism, has been the progenitor of most mixed heritage since, as the saying goes, "We're Here Because You Were There."

For years, I've wanted to make a t-shirt that reads "War Baby/Love Child" on the front, and "What Are You?" on the back. The "What Are You?" T-shirt has been made, I think several times over, by various mixed heritage student groups. The "War Baby/Love Child" t-shirt may never be made by a collective of mixed people, because it brings up painful stereotypes that too many of us have had to counteract. The problem is, people who assume our mothers are Asian women in a war-torn country, and our fathers are American military personnel, too often have a cinematic vision of what that means (picture: Rambo holding a beautiful Vietnamese village girl, whom he loves, in his muscle-bound arms as she dies; or, more likely, picture: Asian bar girl, any ethnicity, dressed lewdly, approaching soldiers with dollar signs in her eyes, "Me love you long time; suckee suckee; me so horny, soldier boy.") They picture desperate/amoral women, or perhaps innocent (but still sexually available) peasant victims. They picture lovely geishas (WW II, Japan) or Korean bar girls (Korean War) or Vietnamese bar girls (Vietnam War) or Filipina camp girls (U.S. military bases in the Philippines) or Chamorro bar girls (U.S. military occupation of Guam) or Hawaiian (Native and mixed Asian) bar girls (U.S. military occupation of Hawaii). Will they now picture Afghan and Iraqi bar girls (in full "I Dream of Jeannie" harem girl fantasy ensemble)? The picture tends to blur because, after 100 years of U.S. military actions, colonialism, and imperialism in Asia and the Pacific (and the importation of labor from Japan, Korea, the Philippines, and China to Hawaii, for good measure) maybe we've begun to all look the same. But what if our parents did meet this way—what then? Does that mean the questioner knows something about our families that they didn't know before? Are they any closer to the truth of our lives?

And even when our parents met in college (as mine did at the University of Hawaii, Maui, in 1968), our history is also the history of war, but it is also the history of our struggle for liberation, social justice and human rights. War Babies/Love's Children: What Are You?

My own family's history may not have been as directly affected by war as some, but neither can it be divorced from this larger global story. My mother's family did not immigrate from Southern China, as did so many in the 1850s–1880s, to the United States, Latin America, South America, Canada, South-East Asia, or Africa. Those that did mostly left because of the wars, poverty, and starvation caused by the Opium Wars waged by Europe and the U.S. from the 1830s–60s to get China to open its borders to the Opium trade being pushed especially by Britain (opium being grown, of course, in the British colonies) to satisfy the need to rectify the trade imbalance caused by European desires for silk, tea, and spices from China.

My mother, the daughter of a wealthy Shanghainese merchant, was one of the many young children handed through a window of "the last train to leave Shanghai" in 1950 before the Communists came (I'm still not sure if this is something she truly remembers or something she saw in a movie). She was raised in Hong Kong and, as had many immigrants before her, decided to come to the U.S. to seek out a different life. My mother did not have to pay a smuggler, nor was she tricked into prostitution or indentured labor. Unlike many other immigrants, she came from a life of relative privilege. She had servants, a nanny, and went to private school. She saw little of her parents, however, and found the life-style of her family stifling and hypocritical. Her parents seemed concerned only with making money and keeping up appearances, so, when she was sixteen, my mother-the-mischievous, asked her father, casually, if he would send her to school abroad, just as her brothers had gone to Sydney and London, if she could get into a school in America.

My mother was a trickster. She had already applied for and been accepted to a private girls' school in Boston; when her father humored her apparent impulse by saying, "of course," she promptly handed him her acceptance letter and demanded he follow through with his promise.

A few years later, after a year freezing at Michigan State, my mother had had enough of cold weather and decided to live out her fantasy by transferring to the University of Hawaii. My father had also done his time in the cold—a year at Seattle University following a lifetime of living near Seattle (his grandfathers, one from Sweden and one from Greece, had settled there with his grandmothers, both multi-generational European Americans: one Scottish and Pennsylvania Dutch, the other English and German). My father was a hippie. It was because he saw himself as a member of the counter culture, that, as he puts it in his version of our family history, a video titled "When We Were Golden," he had to marry his "Chinese girlfriend."

This is where the "Love Child" thing comes in. My dad was/is a white liberal. His family, in 1968, was so "cosmopolitan" that they had no problem with him marrying a Chinese woman. (Nor, for that matter, did my mother's family have any problem with her marrying a white man; in fact, two of her brothers married white women, while my other uncle, Robert, married a woman who is French-Vietnamese.). Perhaps all this gentility was due to the fact that both families share a similar upper-middle class background.

In any case, my father had the luxury of marrying his "Chinese girlfriend" because, as he put it, he'd never tried it before (in a case of the importance of clarifying your referent, I've never been sure if by "it" he meant marriage, or Chinese). My mother's motives were more maternal and less "anti-establishment." Eating a bowl of noodle soup one day, she glanced down and saw, not her own reflection, but a vision of her daughter: me. She saw my father at a party and thought, "We'll make beautiful children together." The marriage didn't last long, so it turned out to be just the one child. Origin myths being what they are, however, there is of course more to the story.

The term "Love Child" must be applied loosely in my case. Insofar as it labels me the children of hippies (or really, just hippie-singular, as I don't think my mother every really embraced the vegetarianism or the Sikh Master or the LSD), the label "Love Child" is accurate. Whether my parents ever really loved each other is certainly open to debate. It is fair to say that they were excited about the idea of doing something socially unexpected. My father's second wife was Chicana, and he has prided himself on being open minded and dating women "from around the world" and "of every race." My mother's story is also not just about love, however. In my mid 20s, I started to ask her questions about her history. After learning something about Asian American history, and learning about the high rates of intermarriage for Asian American women, I asked my mother if she had married my father at least partially because it would make her more accepted here in America. Her answer? "Duh!" (she'd been spending a little too much time with my teenage brother). "Of course," she said, sounding a little irritated at my clueless-ness. "I was an immigrant, a foreigner. I had no family here, no support. After ten years of English lessons in Hong Kong, when I came here I still couldn't understand anything anyone said to me. What was I? Just a cute Chinese girl—at best. At worst, well—you know. Walking down the street with your father, I might be accepted. I might be seen as just a little bit more Americanized. They might assume I spoke English."

Then, as an aside, she added something that shook me: "And with you. Just holding your hand, even without your father, that made me more American. You made me more American." When she told me this my mind raced in circles; we are always thought to think about our identity in terms of our ancestors—we are their creations, their descendants. We *are* the sum of what they *were*. But here was my mother telling me that I had made her who she was; she was at this point in time identifying herself no longer as Chinese, but as a Chinese American—because America is where her children had been born. And then I wondered: when my Swedish/Scottish grandmother showed me proudly around Seattle, saying, "This is Wei Ming, this is my granddaughter," did my identity change hers in a kind of reverse-inheritance? When my father sometimes introduced me to his dates, what was I changing about his identity? What did my existence say, retroactively, about my ancestors? I am the tree that grows from their roots; but I am a hybrid, I am the unexpected mutation. I am not the answer to the question they may have been asked when they got married: "What About the Children?" I am my own question, my own inquiry into how all of this: love, war, sex, power shapes who we are and the world we live in.

War Babies: White Side/Chinese Side

And, to come back around to the beginning, I must look again at our myth of origins: War—because it *is* also the story of my family. As I mentioned earlier, my Uncle Robert married a woman, Annick, my Auntie Nickie, who is the child of a French military officer and a Vietnamese mother, a native of Da Nang. I am reasonably certain her parents would never have met had it not been for the French colonial occupation of "Indochina." I'm also fairly certain that she would never have met my uncle if she were not of mixed heritage. Unlike her siblings of two Vietnamese parents, Auntie Nickie was able, at age eighteen, to leave Vietnam for Japan. Eventually, she found her way to Bangkok and worked at a bank, where she met my Uncle Robert. Their children, my three cousins, have been educated at French schools in Bangkok and boarding schools in Sydney (the family tradition continued). I've bugged my cousins about their identity. After saying, "I don't know, I've never really thought about it," they admit they don't feel particularly Vietnamese. They know they are not French, although culturally they feel connected because of their education. They are Chinese, but only in the way that so many people in the world outside of China and Taiwan are Chinese (for more on that, read the excellent collection by Ien Ang, *On Not Speaking Chinese*). They actually consider themselves Thai, but not really Thai, since they have a fake Thai surname (a law in Thailand for citizenship purposes) and they do sometimes use their Thai personal names in addition to their French personal names.

All my cousins on my mother's side of the family are mixed, except for the latest addition, who is "pure" Shanghainese, according to his father, my Uncle Rudolf. I say, "my mother's side" though I have just as often called it, "my Chinese side." Inaccurately, as it turns out—because it could also be called my "very mixed side." But things change, and sometimes it takes our minds a while to catch up. I'm the eldest of all my cousins, so for a time it made sense to call it, "my Chinese side," and this is often how other multiple heritage people refer to their families: by sides, as though it were a chess game. And as though their families were color-coded.

My "white side" is also a fallacy. For one thing, I'm part of that family, too, so, because I'm not white it can't be white, either. But for another thing, my Korean cousin comes from my "white side." Yes, this is another war story.

My Swedish/Scottish/Pennsylvania Dutch grandmother's cousin was a military officer during the Korean War. He met a Korean woman, and married her, and adopted her son from her marriage to a Korean man. My cousin, Tae-ji, is a Korean transracial adoptee. As it happens, my grandmother's cousin didn't have much other family, so he ended up moving to the Seattle area to be close to someone. And who knows, maybe it was because of "Asian" me that he and his family felt more comfortable with my grandmother than with his other relatives. I know that he and his wife enjoyed coming to family gatherings if they knew my mother and I would be there. We (and only we) would eat, with relish, their homemade pickled daikon. My Korean cousin, Tae-ji, is one of tens of thousands of Koreans who have been transracially adopted, mostly by European Americans. My Auntie Nickie is one of tens of thousands of Eurasians and Amerasians to emerge from half a century of imperialism and war in Vietnam.

We cannot ignore the truth of the War Baby stereotype, just as we cannot ignore the Hollywood-driven fallacies of that image. War Babies and Love Children are what we are, but we can just as well say these things are what the world is, because without these histories of war we would not be the world we are now. American middle-class prosperity, free from war, is a myth we cannot afford.

I will wear a t-shirt that says, "War Baby/Love Child" and on the back, "Ask Me!" because as long as I have hated being asked the dreaded questions, I have also always wanted to tell my answers.

Hapa: Language, Identity and Power

The very success of the word "Hapa" has been in some ways its downfall. What I mean to say is that the word "Hapa" as it is used now may never be able to "shift" back to *only* meaning what it once meant: a Native Hawaiian word meaning mixed or part or half. Paul Spickard writes that he sympathizes "with resentments some Hawaiian may have at their word being appropriated by Asian Americans. But," he continues, "that is the nature of language. It morphs and moves. It is not anyone's property" (262). However, I would argue that this is not merely a question of trying to hold on to a word that, like many words used in the English language, that have been adopted, assimilated, or appropriated. This is a question of power. Who has the power or right to use language? Who has the right to define language? Native Hawaiians, in addition to all of the other ways that their sovereignty has been abrogated, lost for many years the right to their own language through oppressive English-language education. Given this history and given the contemporary social and political reality of Hawaii, the appropriation of this one word has a significance deeper than many Asian Americans are willing to recognize. To have this symbolic word used by Asians, particularly by Japanese Americans, as though it is their own, might in fact symbolically mirror the way Native Hawaiian land was first taken by European Americans, and is now owned by European Americans, Japanese and Japanese Americans and other Asian American ethnic groups that numerically and economically dominate Native Hawaiians in their own land. In "Foregrounding Native Nationalisms: A Critique of Antinationalist Sentiment in Asian American Studies," Candice Fujikane argues that Asian Americans are "settlers" in Hawaii, and therefore "support American colonialism" (76) even while trying to fight racism and discrimination in a "colonial context" (80). She defines the term "settler" in opposition to "native," and argues that Asian Americans "refuse to see themselves as the beneficiaries of [the U.S.] colonial system" (84). Although Fujikane does not here specifically mention the use of the word Hapa by Asian Americans, her argument is certainly in line with the critique that Asian Americans have wrongfully appropriated the term in a way that disenfranchises Native Hawaiians from their culture.

On www.realhapas.com, Lana Robbins argues, "Today's rape of the Hawaiian language also implies that the Hawaiian language means nothing and thus the Hawaiian people are nothing." Robbins argues,

> The raping of Hawaii continues with a new group of colonizers, the California Wanna Be Hapa. As colonizers, California Wanna Be Hapas raped from Hawaiian Hapas their very identity, culture, and history and called it their own. These colonizers justified their illegal actions by creating organizations such as Hapa Issues Forum and other "Hapa" online forums. They gained allies from elite mixed Eurasians who like California Wanna Be Hapas, stole their term from the wartime and colonial Eurasians while stomping on the rights of Amerasians and Hawaiian Hapas.

My response to first hearing this protest was to say, "But I like the word Hapa; look at everything it has done for us." I was also defensive: my experience of being mixed had never felt like a privileged position. It was a difficult thing, often about feeling rejection, exclusion, and racism, from within my own families and my "own" Chinese and White communities. Becoming "Hapa" felt like a refuge from feelings of exclusion and alienation. I didn't want to give "Hapa" up. I remembered how hard it was just to get people to use it. When I first began using the word in 1992, I encountered Korean, Chinese and Filipino people of mixed heritage who objected to using the word Hapa because they thought it was a Japanese term. They didn't want to feel colonized by the Japanese language the way their ancestors had been colonized by Japan. When I informed these people that the word was Native Hawaiian in origin, they then gladly adopted it for themselves. Native Hawaiians have never colonized anyone. When criticism against Asian Americans using the term "Hapa" first started being raised strongly in 2002, I realized that the fact that Native Hawaiians had never colonized anyone, and that is therefore why mixed heritage Asian Americans are comfortable using the word, was a sign of the relative power of Asian Americans in this context. Maybe, I started to think, the word "Hapa" was a colonizing violence in which I was actively participating. At a 2003 talk at UC Berkeley I mentioned my increasing concerns about using the word Hapa. I was very surprised when a young man in the audience became visibly upset at the suggestion that the word Hapa might be somehow taken away from him. It meant so much to him for the same reasons it once meant so much to me—it provides a sense of community and identity in one simple word.

In other words, quite possibly, the word "Hapa," which I had been so happy to wear because of the sense of identity and community it gave me, might have to be destroyed—or like Frodo's ring, which was forged in the fires of Mt. Doom—returned to the point of origin to be re-shaped. I say this knowing that the word can never be again what it once was. There is a nostalgia here that cannot be satisfied even if everyone were to stop using the word "Hapa" to refer to non-Native Hawaiian mixed Asians. But while I certainly do not have the power to fling this word into a "Mt. Doom" of linguistic destruction, I do feel responsible to participate in the dialogue. I have been silent on this issue for too long, perhaps hoping that it would go away, so I could keep "my" word.

The controversy has not gone away, it has only grown stronger, and it is time for me—and other mixed heritage Asian Americans—to recognize that when we use the word "Hapa" it causes some people pain. What is so troubling about this is that the word "Hapa" was chosen because it was the only word we could find that did not really cause us pain. It is not any of the Asian words for mixed Asian people that contain negative connotations either literally (e.g. "children of the dust," "mixed animal") or by association (Eurasian). And it avoids the confused identity and the Black-White dichotomy implied by English phrases (like mixed blood, biracial). It was adopted to enhance an Asian-focus to our mixed identity, thereby allowing us to use the word to participate more fully in our

Asian American communities, and, as I mentioned earlier, is a word that allows us to band together. Individually, as some fraction of a larger ethnic community, Filipino mestizos or Japanese haafus, are relatively small in number. Collectively, as Asian Americans of mixed heritage, we are either second or fourth[6] in terms of position in the overall Asian American population.

Languages grow and evolve, and how they do so reveals the traces of power—but is it our lot to merely record and uncover those changes? Or is it our responsibility to shape those changes? I have to acknowledge that, through my work with Hapa Issues Forum, and as a writer and an educator, I have contributed to spreading the use of the word Hapa by Asian Americans, and I thus feel responsible in part for the current contention.

I presented an earlier version of this paper in November, 2007, at a talk at Occidental College. At the end of my two hours of sharing my research and my series of "Hapa Poems," a young woman who identified herself as Native Hawaiian and Japanese American, told me that my use of the word Hapa felt like a violence—like something was being taken away from her—another piece of Hawaii, another piece of Native Hawaiian culture and identity. She reminded me that I am part of this problem, that I am responsible and have influence and power in this dialogue. I remembered how, in the early 1990s at UC Santa Barbara, I had joyfully and eagerly talked many people into using the word "Hapa;" and I realized that she was right, I do have a responsibility. So here is an attempt to send

---

6. In my 2003 article, "A Community Based on Shared Difference" for the *The New Face of Asian America*, I defined "hapa" as Asian Americans and Pacific Islander Americans of both mixed race and mixed ethnicity, and based on this definition, added up the Census categories and came up with the determination that "hapas would rank second-largest, behind only the Chinese population" (115). Eric Hamako, defining "mixed Asians" as being of partial Asian ancestry and of another race (i.e. not including Pacific Islanders and not including those of mixed ethnic heritage—eg. Chinese and Japanese), has determined the number of "mixed Asians" to be fourth largest among Asian American communities (materials for Mixed Asian Workshop, Association of Asian American Studies Conference, Chicago, April 16, 2008).

"Hapa," which I have seen as my word of self-empowerment, back into the fire, perhaps to be re-forged to serve the community for which it was originally intended—people of mixed Native Hawaiian heritage. I can no longer use a word to empower myself that in the process dis-empowers—even oppresses—others.

Conclusion

Finding another label that works as well as "Hapa" did to draw together our community and create a sense of shared identity seems an impossible task; even now we are dis-aggregating Pacific Islander Americans from Asian Americans, meaning the unifying label "API" (Asian/Pacific Islander) is being dismantled. How can we create community without these collective terms? Should we even try to? Dr. Marianne Maruyma Halpin, the self-identified "White mother of Hapa children," reminded me, after reading an early draft of this essay, that "a name, to work, needs to be something loved." Any name we choose for ourselves must be loved the way my mother loved me through the name she gave me. With that in mind, I suggest that we need to find a name we can all love calling ourselves because it empowers us to be fully ourselves and because it also causes no one else any pain. The name we choose must be loved because it empowers all the marginalized members of our communities— which, let us not forget, includes mixed heritage Native Hawaiians. As we remove this self-imposed label and prepare to replace it with another, let us use re-positionable glue. There will be times when we need the labels to stick, but we must not let them stick us up— we need to know when to let them go, when to recreate them. For now, I will be calling myself a "mixed Asian American"—I don't love this name yet—the abbreviation is "MAA," which isn't exactly euphonious—and I certainly hope we can create something better soon, but for now, I'm just happy to not be mis-using "Hapa." I'm looking forward to working with the poets, writers and dreamers of our community to find another word that gives mixed Asians our own safe space and also locates us firmly within the borders of Asian America.

References

Ang, Ien. 2001. *On Not Speaking Chinese: Living Between Asia and the West.* New York: Routledge.

Espiritu, Yen Le. 1992. *Asian American Panethnicity: Bridging Institutions and Identities.* Temple University Press.

Fujikane, Candace. 2005. "Foregrounding Native Nationalisms: A Critique of Antinationalist Sentiment in Asian American Studies." In *Asian American Studies After Critical Mass,* ed. Kent A. Ono. Blackwell: Malden, MA.

Halpin, Marianne Maruyama. Personal email, 11/20/07.

Hamako, Eric. 2008. Mixed Asian Workshop with Wei Ming Dariotis and Farzana Nayani, presented at Association of Asian American Studies Conference, Chicago, April 16.

"Hapa." Wikipedia. Retrieved 5/8/08.

Hara, Marie. 1999. "Negotiating the Hyphen," introduction, *Intersecting Circles: the voices of Hapa Women in Poetry and Prose.* Hara and Keller, eds. Honolulu: Bamboo Ridge.

Keller, Nora Okja. 1999. "Circling 'Hapa,'" introduction, *Intersecting Circles: the voices of Hapa Women in Poetry and Prose.* Hara and Keller, eds. Honolulu: Bamboo Ridge.

Kina, Laura. Personal email, 11/30/07.

Robbins, Lana. www.realhapas.com, retrieved 11/15/07.

Root, Maria P.P. 2003. "Bill of Rights for Racially Mixed People," *Multiracial Child Resource Book: Living Complex Identities,* Maria P.P. Root and Matt Kelley, eds. Seattle: Mavin Foundation.

Spickard, Paul. 2006. "Afterword." In *Part Asian, 100% Hapa* by Kip Fulbeck. Chronicle Books.

Thompson, Beverly Yuen. 1999. *The Politics of Bisexual/Biracial Identity: A study of bisexual and mixed race women of Asian/Pacific Islander Descent.* Reno: That Damn Book! and Money to Authors Ink. Publishing.

Tolkien, J.R.R. 1954–55. *The Lord of the Rings trilogy.* London: Allen and Unwin.

Tran, Truong. Personal communication, San Francisco, 4/20/06.

Williams, Teresa Kay and Cynthia Nakashima, George Kitahara Kich and G. Reginald Daniel. 1996. "Being Different Together in the University Classroom: Multiracial Identity as Transgressive Education" in *The Multiracial Experience: Racial Borders ad the New Frontier*. Ed. Maria P.P. Root. Thousand Oaks: Sage Publications.

Chapter 4

What about the Children? Exploring Misconceptions and Realities about Mixed-Race Children

Tracey A. Laszloffy & Kerry Ann Rockquemore

The contemporary media's fascination with mixed-race politicians, athletes, musicians, and celebrities suggests that the growing multiracial population has not only captured the public imagination, but also gained a degree of acceptance and legitimacy. Yet, beyond the idealized media images and projections that the U.S. is entering a post-racial future lie the stubbornly persistent problems of race and racism. While interracial marriages have steadily increased over recent decades, interracial couples continue to face overt resistance to their unions from friends, family, and their respective communities. One of the most consistent concerns that family members raise to dissuade individuals from marrying someone of a different race is *"what about the children?"* (Dalmage, 2000).

Embedded in this oft-posed question is a whole host of historically-rooted misconceptions, flawed assumptions, and negative stereotypes about mixed-race children that stand in stark contrast to the harmonious images of interracial families portrayed in the media. In this chapter, we explore two of the most common misconceptions: 1) that mixed-race children inevitably suffer from irreconcilable confusion about their racial identity and 2) that mixed-race children are doomed to a life of tragedy because they experience double rejection (e.g., from both blacks and whites). Based on the findings from empirical research published over the past three decades, we know that some mixed-race children experience confusion about their racial identity, but most develop a clear sense of who they are, even when others may be confused about their race and/or fail to validate their racial identity. We also know that some mixed-race children face double rejection, but these encounters in and of themselves are far less important to healthy identity development than the extent to which children have been prepared to expect, manage, and externalize these experiences.

The extent to which identity confusion and double rejection are problems for mixed-race children depends largely on the racial socialization they receive at home and the expectations that caregivers, families and social service providers have about their racial identity development. When families provide healthy racial socialization, their children develop the clarity, confidence and resources to manage challenges they may encounter in the world at large. This occurs when parents have a clear understanding about race, racism, and the unique process of racial identity development for mixed-race children and adolescents. Because families play such a key role in racial identity development, we conclude by examining the influence of parental factors on the racial socialization of mixed-race children.

Misconception #1:
Doomed to Identity Confusion

Despite ideological, cultural, political, and legal barriers against interracial unions, Americans have been crossing the color line throughout our country's history (Davis, 1991). Whether forced or voluntary, these cross-racial encounters have produced mixed-race children whose racial identity challenges the most fundamental understanding about race: that racial groups are biologically real and mutually exclusive. The most taboo of these unions—that between Blacks and Whites—clearly illustrates the problem of racial classification because the two groups have a history of institutional and ideological oppression (slavery, segregation, and white supremacy), and the most explicit and rigid rules of inclusion and exclusion. In the American context, the status of having both Black and White parents imposes an identity conflict because society forces a choice between two racial groups and assumes that children can belong to one (and only one) group. This *externally-imposed* status-conflict has led many to mistakenly assume that mixed-race children: (1) are *internally* confused (as a personality trait rather than a status conflict), (2) must accept the identity of the lower-status group per the racist one-drop rule, and (3) cannot resolve their inherent racial identity conflict.

Reality: Racial Identity Varies and Can Change over Time

The term "identity" refers to the way we understand ourselves in relation to others and our social environment. Our identities are constructed through a *reflexive* process involving interactions between ourself and others in our social world (e.g., people in our families, schools, neighborhoods, and houses of worship). While the parameters of our racial identities are structurally constrained by macro-level forces (Omi and Winant, 1986), as individuals, our identities include an element of personal agency so that they are "not simply imposed on individuals, but are achieved through interaction, presentation, and manipulation" (Storrs, 1999, p. 200). For mixed-race children, racial identity development is a dynamic process of evolving, developing, and adjusting their self-understanding throughout the life course in ways that respond to a real set of external-imposed constraints.

In contrast to the misconception of irreconcilable identity confusion, researchers have found that most mixed-race people have a great deal of clarity about their racial identities. Using various methodologies and data sets, it has been repeatedly documented that racial identity varies among mixed-race people in *patterned* and *consciously chosen* ways (Kilson, 2001; Renn, 2004; Rockquemore, 1999; Wallace, 2001). Some mixed-race people identify exclusively with the race of only one of their parents, others blend their parent's races to create a hybrid identity, others shift between several different racial identities depending on where they are and who and they are interacting with, and still others refuse any racial identity whatsoever and describe themselves as "human."

The pattern of variation has been most thoroughly documented among mixed-race people with one Black and one White parent where some develop an exclusively "Black" identity (Storrs 1999), others an exclusively "White" identity (Rockquemore and Arend, 2003; Twine, 1997), still others create an integrated "biracial," "multiracial," or "mixed" identity (Gibbs and Hines, 1992), some shift between "Black," "White," and "biracial" identities, depending on the racial composition of the group they are interacting within (Harris and Sim, 2002; Rockquemore, 1999), and some refuse any racial designation whatsoever (Rockquemore and Brunsma, 2001). While variation in racial identity has been most comprehensively documented among mixed-race people with one Black and one White parent, that variation has also been observed among other mixed-race groups (Brunsma, 2005; Herman, 2004; Kana'iaupuni and Liebler, 2005; King, 2000; Lee and Bean, 2004; Wright et al., 2003; Xie and Goyette, 1997).

Another important and consistently documented fact that simultaneously challenges and contributes to the misconception of identity confusion is that it's common for mixed-race people to change their racial identity over their lifetime. This differs from conceptualizations of single-race identity because identity development for mixed-race people doesn't occur in a predictable, linear fashion. Gatson (2003) and Renn (2004) describe how their mixed-race respondent's racial identities shift and adapt as they experience social, material, cultural, and economic changes in their lives. Hitlin, Brown, and Elder (2006) have documented the shifting of racial identity over time by mapping the longitudinal "pathways of racial self-identification" in a nationally representative sample of fourteen to eighteen-year-olds. They found that mixed-race youth are four times more likely to switch their racial identity than to consistently report the same identification over the observed time periods. While change occurs, it varies between diversifying, consolidating, or maintaining multiracial self-identification.

Certainly, mixed-race children and adolescents face forced-choice situations in which they are literally forced into self-designating as a member of one racial group (e.g., government forms, application forms). Even the illusion of the "check all that apply" instructions on the census end up with government bureaucrats re-aggregating the data to force multiple-race respondents into a single-race schema for analysis. Yet, the emergent research suggests that there is a difference between choosing a racial *label* or *box* on a form and being forced to choose a single racial *identity*. David Brunsma (2005) characterizes this difference as one between "private and public identities" in which mixed-race adolescents and young adults exhibit a strategic deployment of racial identity in the public sphere in ways that are conscious, intentional, and far from the age-old stereotype of confusion (Rockquemore and Arend, 2003).

The notion that mixed-race people suffer from an irreconcilable confusion about their racial identity is tied more broadly to the problem of rigidly defined and narrow rules around what constitutes a healthy and legitimate racial identity for this population. For decades, social scientists, clinicians, and statisticians have grappled over what defines the "healthy" or "correct" racial identity for mixed-race children. Before the 1980s researchers (operating on the assumption of the one-drop rule) argued that the healthy choice for children with one Black and one White parent was "Black." By the mid 1980s multiracial activists challenged this view and openly questioned the racist logic underlying the one-drop rule. Their public resistance to census categories coincided with the emergence of new theoretical models that assumed the only "healthy" racial identification was "biracial."

While each of these positions argued for a different outcome, they shared a common belief that there is one (and only one) "right" or "healthy" way for mixed-race children to racially self-identify. As such, anyone who did not fit within these narrowly defined options was deemed to be suffering from confusion, internalized racism, and/or over-identification with one of their parents. However, study after study indicates that multiracial children identify in lots of different ways and that their racial identities evolve and change throughout the life-course (Root, 1990). In short, there are many different ways that mixed-race children and adolescents understand who they are and where they fit in our racialized social world. No one identity choice is more or less healthy than another. Instead, the intricate dance between structure and agency that is so clear among the mixed-race population begs deeper questions such as: What is "correct?" For whom and for what purpose is it "correct?" What is "healthy?" Is racial identity fluid and pliable? And if so, what does this mean to the evaluation of mixed-race children's mental health?

We have argued elsewhere that the key to health is not the racial category individuals use to describe their identity but rather how and why they arrive at that choice (Rockquemore and Laszloffy, 2005). In other words, we are less concerned with the *label* a child uses and focus instead on the *pathway* he or she travels to arrive at that label. There are many possible pathways that can lead to the same racial identification or label. Focusing on the pathway enables a clearer analysis of the factors that contribute and cause healthy versus unhealthy racial identity. We define "healthy" as a genuine acceptance of the complex reality of having parents of different races. Our view of "unhealthy" is any process of self-understanding that is steeped in denial. Consequently, the degree of health reflected in a particular racial identity is defined by how much a child accepts or denies having parents of different races.

Acceptance has both cognitive and emotional dimensions. It is not enough to be able to acknowledge as an intellectual reality that one has parents of two different races. Rather, it is important to be able to manifest psychological and emotional recognition of this truth. Genuine acceptance occurs when a child has integrated the fact of mixed-race ancestry into her sense of self and has a peaceful relationship with it, rather than a reactive and unresolved relationship with that status. In its most extreme form, denial involves complete disavowal of having mixed-race ancestry and/or an idealization of one racial group accompanied by demonization of the other. In its milder form, individuals may intellectually accept the fact of having parents of two different races while psychologically struggling to integrate this reality into their self-concept.

The popular misconception that mixed-race people are racially confused is steeped in fundamental misunderstandings about race and racial categories, the unique process of racial identity development for mixed-race children (that differs from Whites and Blacks), and essentialist ideas about what constitutes health. While the historically-rooted rules of racial group classification have constrained the identity options for mixed-race children, the assumption that "Black" or "biracial" are the only legitimate identity options, and that these identities must remain fixed and unchanging throughout an individual's life, simply are not consistent with the research literature. In fact, many different identity options exist and are utilized by multiracial people. Even more important than the actual labels mixed-race people adopt are the pathways they travel to arrive at their choices. Recent research indicates that while some mixed-race people experience racial identity confusion, most do not. Instead, the norm is that mixed-race people have a clear sense of their racial identification and even among those whose identity changes over time, their changes are perceived as positive developments in their self-understanding and maturation.

Misconception #2:
Doomed by Double Rejection

It is all too commonly assumed that mixed-race children will have difficulty being accepted by others because of their "in-betweeness." In other words, many who ask "what about the children?" are really wondering how a mixed-race child can ever be fully accepted by children of either race as an authentic group member and worry that they will be destined to live their life as a permanent outsider because they are "neither fish nor fowl."

Reality: Acceptance and Comfort Require Contact

Any child's acceptance by others as an in-group member is largely determined by their childhood experiences with members of that group. Specifically, the level of closeness a child feels to members of any racial group depends upon: 1) the racial composition of his/her social network (school, neighborhood, friends), 2) the type of interactions he/she has in that network, and 3) his/her physical appearance. In studies of mixed-race college students with one Black and one White parent, Rockquemore and Brunsma (2002) found that those who grew up in predominately Black neighborhoods, attended mostly Black schools, and had mostly Black friendship networks in childhood were likely to develop an exclusively "Black" identity. Alternatively, students who lived in predominately white neighborhoods, attended white schools and had mostly White friendship networks were more likely to develop a "biracial" identity. This difference is, at least in part, due to the fact that Black and White communities have different ways of understanding the social location of mixed-race children, what it means to be Black and/or whether "biracial" is a legitimate racial identity. In this way, a child's social context exerts an important influence on the parameters of racial identity that are available, accepted, rejected, or contested.

While it is important to understand the relationship between the racial composition of mixed-race children's social networks and their racial identities, it is also critical to consider the *types of interactions* they have with others in those networks. The experiences children have of being accepted or rejected by others shape how connected they feel to various groups of people. When peers and friends communicate messages that affirm and accept a child's chosen racial identity, that child is more likely to embrace and build upon that choice (Rockquemore and Laszloffy, 2005). Conversely, if peers and friends are critical or reject a child's self-identification, he/she will be more likely to modify and reject his/her self-definition in an attempt to solicit greater social approval. The names children get called on the playground, how they are teased, and the racialized insults that are exchanged in arguments have the effect of situating and placing children in relation to one another. These daily micro-interactions and sensitive relational dynamics directly shape mixed-race children's sense of self, comfort, and connection to individuals (and groups) as well as how they come to think about and present themselves racially.

In addition to the racial composition of a child's social environment and the types of interactions they have in that context, his/her physical appearance is critically important to their sense of belonging to a racial group. This is the case because physical appearance is the primary cue for racial group membership in the United States and based on historical circumstances, our society associates specific physical characteristics with racial group membership (Omi and Winant, 1986). Mixed-race children vary widely in their physical appearance (even within the same family) but the impact that appearances have on their racial identity is fairly consistent.

Racial identity is a socially validated self-understanding and therefore it must be true to how we see ourselves *and* be validated by others. A bi-directional process occurs between how a child sees him/herself and how others see him/her. For example, when a mixed-race child with one Black and one White parent appears "Black" and develops a racial identification that corresponds with the socially constructed meanings associated with their physical appearance (Black), there is a perfect correlation between how they see themselves and how others see them. By contrast, a child who appears "White," but self-identifies as "Black," may encounter some resistance from blacks because of the disconnection between her chosen racial identity and her physical appearance. Because of the historical norms established by the one-drop rule (if you have even a drop of "Black blood" you cannot be White), those who assert a "White" identity but who physically appear "Black" are likely to encounter the greatest amount of resistance and rejection. Finally, those children with an ambiguous appearance inevitably must grapple with the reality that their racial identity is not immediately clear to most people. While a "Black" or "biracial" identity is likely to be accepted by others once it is proclaimed, a "White" identity is more likely than not to be met with rejection (Rockquemore and Brunsma, 2001).

The dynamics of acceptance and rejection of mixed-race children by children of different racial groups is also heavily influenced by the child's gender (Rockquemore, 2002). The historically-rooted interaction of racial and gender oppression manifests today in terms of skin color stratification (Hunter, 2005). During slavery, White slave masters routinely raped Black women, resulting in lighter-skinned offspring and introducing a skin color hierarchy among slaves. Slave masters ruthlessly exploited variations in skin color by favoring lighter-skinned slaves. The privileges that were afforded to those who were lighter contributed to tensions among slaves on the basis of skin color that continue to shape relationships between lighter and darker-skinned black people today, especially among women (Keith and Herring, 1991; Russell, Wilson, and Hall, 1993).

One reason why skin color takes on greater weight among women is because the nature of sexism is such that women are judged more than men on the basis of their physical attributes. Women's beauty strongly impacts how they are valued and socially rewarded (Baker, 1984). Beauty standards lie at the intersection of sexism and racism, dictating that White features (e.g. light skin, blond hair, blue eyes) are "beautiful." This leaves Black women with light skin, light colored or long hair, and green, blue or hazel eyes privileged as more valuable than those with dark skin, kinky or short hair, and brown eyes (Hunter, 2005; Hill-Collins, 1990). Tensions that are centered on physical attributes often arise between girls (and women) of differing complexions.

The strains between lighter and darker-skinned girls create complications for mixed-race girls whose appearances range the phenotypic spectrum: light to dark skin, straight to kinky hair, and every eye color imaginable (Rockquemore and Laszloffy, 2005). Much of that tension is grounded in the issue of identity choice. Irrespective of their complexion, Black girls develop a racial identity as "Black." By contrast, mixed-race girls have the option of adopting a "Black," "biracial," or (in some cases) "White" identity. While often unconscious, Black girls can resent the fact that their mixed-race peers have greater freedom to choose their racial identity. This contributes to the underlying dynamic that privileges light skin and white features, and can strain relationships between Black and mixed-race girls. As Black girls sense mixed-race girls pulling away from Blackness ("I'm *not* Black, I'm biracial!"), they are more likely to become rejecting ("she thinks she's White") which further distances mixed-race girls from their Blackness. Similarly, as mixed-race girls fear or perceive rejection they are more likely to distance themselves from Blackness ("I always have problems with Black girls") thereby pushing away all Black girls based on negative experiences with a few. The cycle continues to spiral during adolescence when the competition for the male attention can become explosive (Rockquemore, 2002). Clearly, perceived rejection and corresponding pain are at the heart of the tension that often exists on both sides of this persistent conflict.

Ultimately, some mixed-race children do encounter rejection from both Whites and Blacks. However, the nature and extent of such rejection depends on a host of factors, some of which have nothing to do with the child, such as the other person's racial attitudes, perceptions, and personal history. Some factors are specific to the child such as her or his physical appearance, racial presentation, and overall familiarity and comfort around people of various races. The impact of such experiences is mitigated by parents' conscious efforts to expose and racially socialize their children to be comfortable around people of different races, provide them with specific tools and skills for handling rejection or discrimination, and support them in being clear and confident in their racial identity, irrespective of others reactions. It's the analytic and discursive tools that parents arm their children with, as opposed to the experiences of rejection themselves, that make the critical difference in how mixed-race children weather the inevitable racialized experiences of interpersonal rejection.

Racial Socialization in Interracial Families

Mixed-race children may experience rejection from Whites and Blacks, they may express confusion about their self-identification, and they may encounter others who are confused about their identity, but these experiences in and of themselves do not doom them to tragedy. It is the kind of racial socialization that mixed-race children experience in their families that shapes how well-adjusted they are and how they respond to the confusion and rejection they may experience. When families provide *effective racial socialization*, children develop a buffer against potentially negative experiences that allow them to develop and assert a clear and confident racial identity even while others may exhibit confusion or rejection. Conversely, *ineffective racial socialization* heightens children's risk of identity confusion and increases their vulnerability to the rejecting and negative messages they receive from others in their environment.

Effective racial socialization consists of creating a climate where children are encouraged to be curious and talk openly about racial issues. It involves an understanding of race, racism, and racial inequalities in the U.S., as well as learning to identify and challenge attitudes and behaviors that perpetuate racial inequality. This occurs by exposing children to a diverse array of people, particularly role models that provide positive representations of people of color, mixed-race people, and white people working for racial equality. Healthy racial socialization teaches children to appreciate the positive and negatives aspects of both Whiteness and Blackness, and it fosters skills for negotiating situations where they may encounter confusion, rejection and/or discrimination (Rockquemore and Laszloffy, 2005). The extent to which parents are able to provide healthy racial socialization is related to three important factors: 1) each individual parent's cross-racial experiences and personal development; 2) the quality of the relationship between parents; and 3) how parents respond to their children's physical appearance. We discuss each of these three factors in turn.

Individual Parental Factors

The experiences parents have had with race, racism, and racial inequality throughout their lives strongly influence how they racially socialize their children. The experiences include the racial attitudes and behaviors parents were exposed to when they were children, the beliefs they developed about racial groups, and their contact with people of varying racial groups. The cumulative effect of cross-racial relationships shapes how parents of mixed-race children think and feel about race and informs the messages they transmit in their daily interactions.

The nature of racial inequality in the U.S. is such that Black families must orient their children to racism and how it creates differential opportunities for Black and White people. In this way, most Black parents understand that it is important to take an active and intentional approach to teaching their children about race relations. Conversely, most White families are not consciously aware of race and the privileges they are afforded by virtue of their Whiteness. Silence in White families sends the message that race is something that relates only to people of color and not them. Moreover, since White supremacist ideology is part of the dominant cultural discourse, most White families collude with this ideology simply by virtue of doing nothing to resist it and thereby maintaining the racial status quo through acts of omission rather than commission. Since racial privilege allows White people to not have to think about or be sensitive to issues of race, most White families tend to be racially unaware and insensitive. This poses a challenge for many White parents of mixed-race children. If they were raised in families that failed to consciously and directly examine matters of race in a progressive way, they tend to be ill-prepared to raise children of color to understand and be responsive to the realities of their racial location.

The frequency and quality of contact that parents have had with members of their own and other racial groups are salient experiences shaping how they racially socialize their children. Because Whites are the dominant racial group in the United States, most people have had extensive contact with White people. But it is entirely possible for White people to have minimal contact with people of color. The extent to which parents have had cross-racial contact is important because it is only through such encounters that one can truly learn about themselves in relations to others. Repeated opportunities to interact with people of different races is critical because in the absence of such experiences, it is too easy to make broad sweeping generalizations about a group based on only a handful of interactions (whether largely positive or negative). When parents have had minimal contact with members of other racial groups, it limits their cultural knowledge and their underlying sense of comfort with members of that group, and that discomfort is easily transmitted to their children. In the interest of providing effective racial socialization, it behooves parents to have frequent, sustained, and meaningful contact with a diverse array of people.

Each of us has a way in which we understand ourselves racially and this influences how we are inclined to approach racial socialization with children. In particular, a parent's stage of racial identity development greatly informs their parenting. Helm's (1995) model of White identity development posits that individuals begin at a primary level that consists of unconscious identification with Whiteness and unquestioned acceptance of stereotypes about racial minorities. As development progresses, individuals enter a conflict stage when their awareness of racial issues grows and they begin to reflect on their Whiteness. This stage involves tension between wanting to conform to majority norms and wanting to support notions of racial and social justice. Feelings of guilt, anger, and depression are common and may lead to hostility toward White culture or conversely, to defensive retreat. Those who evolve to the highest level of development undergo a redefinition of Whiteness that involves taking responsibility to challenge racism and developing a non-racist White identity.

Since most White parents are raised to not think about their Whiteness they tend to suffer from the "invisibility of Whiteness" that leads them to assume race is not their concern. They tend to be unaware of how their values reflect a racial orientation and may aggressively assert that they "don't see color" or are "colorblind." For White parents of mixed-race children, it is important to move beyond the primary stage of racial identity development so they are better able to talk openly and honestly with their children about of the realities of race, racism and racial inequalities. Doing so requires struggling directly with their own racial identity, including working through race-based emotions as a way of advancing beyond defensive anger and debilitating guilt. It is helpful for effective racial socialization when White parents are able to embrace their Whiteness while also being accountable for the unearned benefits of Whiteness.

Black parents also advance through various stages in their racial identity development (Cross, 1991). The primary level is often referred to as the pre-encounter stage that involves a superficial understanding of race and identification with norms of Whiteness. This is followed by an immersion stage that tends to be triggered by experiences with racism that forces individuals to engage more deeply with what it means to be a Black person living in a racist society. Feelings of rage toward Whiteness and racial inequalities are common at this point. While some people remain developmentally stuck at this stage, ideally one evolves towards having a clear, proud sense of being a Black person, balanced with an ability to critically and fairly evaluate Whiteness. At this stage, individuals are able to make distinctions between individual White people and the broader system of White oppression.

Given the nature of the society we live within, all of us internalize messages that teach us to overvalue Whiteness and devalue Blackness. For mixed-race children, it is best when their parents have an advanced understanding of their racial identity that corresponds with being able to critically evaluate the anatomy of race in America and are able to formulate and integrate balanced articulations of Whiteness and Blackness. These capabilities are invaluable assets for parents raising children of all races, but especially for those who are mixed-race. When parents have experiences that expose them to the realities of race and diverse groups of people, learn to talk openly and critically about racial issues, and are evolved in their own racial identity development, they are better positioned to support healthy racial identity development among their mixed-race children. They are able to be effective in their racial socialization because they can help their mixed-race children to explore, interrogate, wrestle with racism and help them to integrate both their Whiteness and their Blackness into a cohesive self-understanding.

The Quality of the Parents' Relationship

All couples' relationships are complex and even the best ones involve struggles that impact parenting. When the unique pressures inherent in interracial relationships are present, creating and maintaining healthy relationships becomes even more challenging. When conflicts arise between parents, children often perceive "sides" that they have to choose between. In interracial families, it is not uncommon for the perception of sides to be racialized. Tracey Laszloffy is a therapist who worked with an interracial family consisting of a black woman named Evelyn, and a white man named Charlie (all names are pseudonyms) in therapy. While not married, Evelyn and Charlie had been a couple for nearly seventeen years and had two teenage daughters named Kea and Julie. After Evelyn discovered Charlie had been having an affair with a White woman she was overwhelmed with rage and hurt. Both daughters were exposed to the strife that had erupted in their parents' relationship, including hearing their mother say that "White men are no good" and "they can't be trusted," while their father said "Black women are too hard to deal with" and "they don't know how to take care of a man." In this family, the girls were trapped between adults who were at war with each other, and this conflict had specific racial messages attached to it. As each of the girls felt their parents vying for their loyalties, they were simultaneously being pushed and pulled in different directions around race, group membership, and identity.

As this example and countless others like it highlight, children can become drawn into parental conflict in ways that affect their developing sense of self. This is true in all families, but in mixed-race families, racial issues can become infused with parental dynamics in ways that specifically influence how children come to think and feel about themselves racially. Consequently, when parents have destructive conflict it is essential that they pay close attention to the ways in which they may unwittingly expose their children to these tensions, racialize their emotions, and in doing so vie for children's racial loyalty.

Parents' Response to Physical Appearance

How parents respond to their children's physical appearance conveys specific messages to children about race that impact how children come to see and feel about themselves racially. In light of the racial hierarchy that organizes the United States, it is not uncommon for parents to display preference for lighter-skinned, "Whiter"-looking children versus darker-skinned, "Blacker"-looking children. Repeatedly telling lighter skinned children how "cute" they are, referring to curly hair as "good hair," and commenting on children's "pretty eyes" (if they are any color other than brown) can send powerful messages about the value associated with physical traits. More often, parents may communicate preference in non-verbal ways via differential treatment of siblings who vary in their physical appearance. In some instances, especially when a parent is darker-skinned and has had negative experiences with rejection, they may express hostility or aggression towards a lighter-skinned child. When this occurs, not only does it powerfully affect how children come to see and feel about themselves racially, it can also complicate and strain sibling relations.

Physical appearance also influences how children and families are perceived outside of their home. All too frequently, strangers make quick and erroneous assumptions about who constitutes a family based on physical appearance. Moreover, assumptions frequently are made based on specific meanings that are attached to particular physical appearances. For example, because people of color are often assumed to be in positions of service to white people, within interracial families, mothers of color are frequently assumed to be nannies to children who appear white. Experiences like these can contribute to feelings of frustration, humiliation, and strain within interracial families that can have a corresponding influence on racial socialization and development.

With respect to racial socialization, it is important for parents to be aware of their own biases and reactions toward particular kinds of physical appearances and to monitor how they respond to their children's physical characteristics in specific ways. It is best of course, when parents demonstrate no overt or subtle preference for (or negativity toward) any particular kind of appearance. And even better is when parents are able to find specifically positive aspects of each of their children's physical qualities to celebrate and admire as beautiful in balanced and equitable ways.

Raising Biracial Children

The changing nature of race relations in post-civil rights America has fundamentally shifted the experiences of multiracial children. Role models such as Tiger Woods, Soledad O'Brien, and Barack Obama abound and communicate new possibilities for mixed-race people, in which a full range of racial identities are acceptable and legitimate. Yet, despite this progress, old stereotypes of confused, rejected, "tragic mulattos" remain fixed in the popular imagination and continue to be trotted out with sincerity to interracial couples as a serious reason why they should not marry and/or start a family.

In this chapter, we have described what researchers know about mixed-race people in order to critically engage the misconceptions of being tragically doomed by virtue of identity confusion and double rejection. While some mixed-race children experience internal confusion, most do not. They construct a broad spectrum of racial identities and adapt as their life circumstances evolve. And while mixed-race people may have encounters with double rejection, *how* they handle these experiences matters to their health and stability. Children who have been socialized in ways that prepare them to manage others' rejection can weather these experiences with minimal negative impact. The critical issue in both cases is the type of racial socialization that families provide. Families are the first place that children learn to think and feel about race, negotiate their racial identities, understand their connection to racial groups, and navigate a social world that claims to be colorblind, yet is replete with individual and institutional racism. The extent to which parents are aware of and sensitive to issues of race and encourage children to openly explore the history and culture of all their racial groups greatly influences the degree to which children come to accept or reject their multiracial status, are clear and confident in their racial identification, and are able to effectively manage experiences with rejection or discrimination.

References

Baker, N. 1984. *The beauty trap*. New York: Franklin Watts.

Brunsma, D.L. 2005. Interracial families and the racial identification of mixed-race children: Evidence from the early childhood longitudinal study. *Social Forces* 84: 1131–1157.

Collins, P. H. 1990. *Black feminist thought*. New York: Routledge.

Cross, W. 1991. *Shades of black*. Philadelphia: Temple University Press.

Dalmage, H. 2000. *Tripping on the color line: Black white multiracial families in a racially divided world*. Piscataway, NJ: Rutgers University Press.

Davis, F. J. 1991. *Who is black?* University Park: Pennsylvania State University Press.

Gatson, S. 2003. On being amorphous: Autoethnography, genealogy, and a multiracial identity. *Qualitative Inquiry* 9: 20–48.

Gibbs, J.T., and A.M. Hines. 1992. Negotiating ethnic identity: Issues for black-white biracial adolescents. In *Racially mixed people in America*, ed. M. Root, 223–238. Newbury Park, CA: Sage.

Harris, D., and J. Sim, 2002. Who is multiracial? Assessing the complexity of lived race. *American Sociological Review* 67: 614–27.

Helms, J.E. 1995. An update of Helms's white and people of color racial identity models. In *Handbook of multicultural counseling*, ed. J. G. Ponterotto, J.M. Casas, L.A. Suzuki, and C.M. Alexander, 181–198. Thousand Oaks, CA: Sage.

Herman, M. 2004. Forced to choose: Some determinants of racial identification in multi-racial adolescents. *Child Development* 75: 730–748.

Hitlin, S. Brown, J.S. and G.H. Elder. 2006. Racial self-categorization in adolescence: Development and social pathways. *Child Development* 77(5): 1298–1308.

Hunter, M. 2005. *Race, gender and the politics of skin tone.* New York: Routledge.

Kana'iaupuni, S. and C. Liebler. 2005. Pondering poi dog: Place and racial identification of multiracial native Hawaiians. *Ethnic and Racial Studies* 28, 687–721.

Keith, V. and C. Herring. 1991. Skin tone stratification in the black community. *American Journal of Sociology* 97: 760–778.

Kilson, M. 2001. *Claiming place: Biracial young adults of the post-civil rights era.* Westport, CT: Bergin & Garvey.

King, R. 2000. Racialization, recognition, and rights: Lumping and splitting multiracial Asian Americans in the 2000 Census. *Journal of Asian American Studies* 3: 191–217.

Lee, J. and F. Bean. 2004. American's changing color lines: Immigration, race/ethnicity, and multiracial identification. *Annual Review of Sociology* 30: 221–242.

Omi, M. and H. Winant. 1986. *Racial formation in the United States from the 1960s to the 1980s.* New York: Routledge.

Renn, K. 2004. *Mixed race students in college: The ecology of race, identity, and community on campus.* Albany, NY: State University of New York Press.

Rockquemore, K.A. 1999. Between black and white: Exploring the biracial experience. *Race and Society* 1: 197–212.

Rockquemore, K.A. 2002. Negotiating the color line: The gendered process of racial identity construction among black/white biracials. *Gender & Society* 16: 485–503.

Rockquemore, K.A. and P. Arend. 2003. Opting for white: Choice, fluidity, and black identity construction in post-Civil Rights America. *Race and Society* 5: 51–66.

Rockquemore, K.A. and D.L. Brunsma. 2001. *Beyond black: Biracial identity in America.* Thousand Oaks, CA: Sage.

Rockquemore, K.A. and D.L. Brunsma. 2002. Socially embedded identities: Theories, typologies, and processes of racial identity among biracials. *The Sociological Quarterly* 43: 335–356.

Rockquemore, K.A. and T. Lazloffy. 2005. *Raising biracial children.* Lanham, MD: Altamira Press.

Root, M. P. P. 1990. Resolving other status: Identity development of biracial individuals. *Women and Therapy* 9: 185–205.

Russell, K., M. Wilson and R. Hall. 1993. *The color complex.* New York: Anchor.

Storrs, D. 1999. Whiteness as stigma: Essentialist identity work by mixed-race women. *Symbolic Interaction* 23: 187–212.

Twine, F.W. 1997. Brown-skinned white girls: Class, culture and the construction of white identity in suburban communities. In *Displacing whiteness: Essays in social and cultural criticism,* ed. R. Frankenberg, 214–243. Durham, NC: Duke University Press.

Wallace, K. 2001. *Relative/outsider: The art and politics of identity among mixed-heritage students.* Westport, CT: Ablex.

Wright, R., S. Houston, M. Ellis, S. Holloway, and M. Hudson, 2003. Crossing racial lines: Geographies of mixed-race partnering and multiraciality in the United States. *Progress in Human Geography* 27: 457–474.

Xie, Y. and K. Goyette. 1997. The racial identification of bi-racial children with one Asian parent: Evidence from the 1990 Census. *Social Forces* 76: 547–70.

Chapter 5

Race and Intimate Partner Violence: Violence in Interracial and Intraracial Relationships

Angela Hattery & Earl Smith

Introduction

In this chapter we examine a particular aspect of intimate partner violence (IPV): that which occurs in interracial relationships. Why study IPV in interracial relationships?

First and foremost, because most of the men and women whom we interviewed as part of a larger book project on intimate partner violence were involved in *intraracial* relationships (Hattery and Smith 2007), but a few of our interview subjects were in fact involved in interracial relationships. These interviews—50 in all—sparked our curiosity about the ways that race dynamics shape IPV, thus allowing us to analyze the utility of the race, class, and gender paradigm in understanding IPV as it occurs in couples of different racial composition.

In order to provide a context for the analysis we begin with a discussion of patterns of interracial relationships in the U.S.

Interracial Relationships

Looking at the big picture, an examination of trends confirms that there has been an overall steady increase in the rates of all interracial marriage (Qian 2005; Wilson, 1987). In 1960, fewer than 4 in 1,000 married couples in the United States were interracial couples. Currently (based on the 2000 U.S. Census), 5.7 percent of married couples and 10.2 percent of cohabiting heterosexual couples were interracial (Simmons & O'Connell 2003). Although still modest overall, interracial marriage has become particularly pronounced among some segments of the population while it remains very uncommon in others (Qian and Lichter 2007). For example, it is important to note that among all interracial marriages, the highest rate by far is White-Asian marriages with the most common arrangement being marriages between White men and Asian women. In fact, currently 50 percent of Asian women are now marrying "out" (U.S. Bureau of the Census, 1999).[1]

With respect to Black-White marriages, we note that these unions are also strongly shaped by the intersection of race and gender. Those involving Black men and non-Black women, for example, have become increasingly more common since the U.S. Supreme Court ruled that laws prohibiting interracial unions are unconstitutional (Kalmijn, 1993). In 1970, fewer than 1.5 percent of married African American men were married to non-Black women, and only 1.2 percent of African American men were married to

---

1. In order to test the stability of the claim that White men are more likely to engage in physical IPV when they are in intraracial relationships as opposed to interracial relationships, we examined the prevalence of physical IPV in relationships between White men and Asian women. There were very few statistically significant differences, but the overall trends confirm our finding in this chapter. With regards to *both* instances of interracial relationships — with African American or Asian female partners — White men are *less violent* when they are in interracial relationships than when they are in intraracial relationships (with White women). Data not shown here. For a summary of the data tables please contact the authors.

White women (U.S. Bureau of the Census, 1972). In comparison, according to census data, by 1990 about 4.5 percent of the nation's married African American men had non-Black spouses, with the majority of these being White women (U.S. Bureau of the Census, 1999).[2] In contrast, marriages between African American women and non-Black men, especially White men, have historically been much less common than intermarriage between African American men and non-Black women. Census data indicate that in 1990 fewer than 2 percent of the country's married African American women had non-Black spouses (U.S. Bureau of the Census, 1999) up from just 0.8 percent in 1970 (U.S. Bureau of the Census, 1972).

Figure 5-1 Trends in Interracial Marriage in the United States 1960–1998

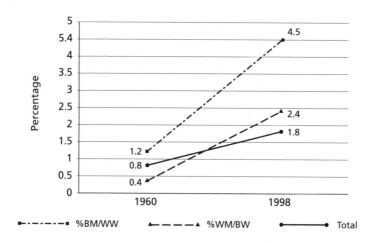

Data from the U.S. Bureau of the Census

In addition, Qian notes that there are other differences in marriages between African Americans and Whites. Though overall

---

2. Wilson explores these trends using a different technique, examining marriage license data (W. J. Wilson, 1987). His analysis confirms the same trend.

African American men receive less education than all other race/ethnic and gender status groups (Hattery & Smith 2007), when they do attain high levels of education they are more likely to marry outside of their race. For example, when White women marry African American men they "marry up" in terms of educational attainment. In other words, there are more pronounced educational differences in marriages between African American men and White women than in *intraracial* marriages of either African Americans or Whites (Qian, 2005). Qian goes on to suggest that this difference in educational attainment can lead to the presumption that White women are taking the best African American men out of the marriage pool, which is consistent with the beliefs that many African American women report (Qian, 2005).

Black-White Intermarriage

Because of the contentious nature of interracial dating and marriage in American society—from early on to now—particularly the African American/White variant of these relationships, there has always been a sort of "odd" curiosity about these couples (Johnson 1970). As a result, we have decades of opinion poll research that examines Americans' attitudes about interracial dating and marriage (Datzman and Brooks 2000).

For example in 1948, when the Supreme Court of California legalized interracial marriage (it was the first state to do so) about 90 percent of American adults opposed interracial marriage. In 1967, about 72 percent of Americans were opposed to interracial marriage. This was the same year that the U.S. Supreme Court, based primarily on the case of Loving v. Virginia,[3] declared unconstitutional all state laws that banned interracial marriages in U.S. states.[4]

Based on our experiences with school desegregation and other major shifts in social life, which provide examples of attitudes lag-

---

3. SUPREME COURT OF THE UNITED STATES, 386 U.S. 952; 87 S. Ct. 1017; 18 L. Ed. 2d 101; 1967 U.S. LEXIS 2065, Mar. 13, 1967.

4. We note that these laws were referred to as anti-miscegenation laws.

ging behind court decisions, it stands to reason then that it wasn't until 1991 that the percent of Americans opposed to interracial marriage became a *minority* for the first time. Yet, the research by Bonilla-Silva and Forman (2000:55) shows that despite the liberalizing of American's views on African American/White unions, there is a big gap between what White Americans say ("I Am Not a Racist, But ..."), and what they do.

> A very high proportion of Whites claim to approve of interracial marriage, friendship with Blacks, and with people of color moving into predominantly White neighborhoods ... However, results based on two non-traditional measures of social distance from Blacks indicate something different.

Bonilla-Silva and Foreman (2000) conclude, based on data from their in-depth interviews, that contrary to the color-blind attitudes of their respondents, most of them actually held very color conscious views.

It is still true that interracial marriage rates, particularly those between African Americans and Whites, are extremely low (less than 5 percent) (Qian and Lichter 2007). Yet, the hold on maintaining boundaries between African Americans and Whites, designed to prevent sexual liaisons, over time results in the uniqueness of these relationships throughout U.S. history.

Furthermore, the relative rarity of interracial couples adds to the perception of the exotic nature of these relationships, prompting these couples to report that they are often the object of intense negative curiosity. Our concern is, does this over-scrutiny from the outside in any way contribute to the violence that comes from within?

Theoretical Framework: Race, Class and Gender

The race, class, and gender framework was largely developed by black and multiracial feminists (Davis, 1983; Zinn 2005; Anderson 2001; Hill-Collins 1994, 2004; King 1988). This theoretical paradigm rests on the assumption that systems of oppression and domination (i.e. patriarchy, capitalism, and racial superiority) exist independently and are woven together in what Baca Zinn and Thornton Dill (2005) refer to as a matrix of domination. They and others argue that many phenomena from child rearing (Hill and Sprague 1999) to the wage gap (Padavic and Reskin, 2002), to incarceration (Hattery and Smith, 2008, Western 2005) and intimate partner violence (Esqueda 2005; Hattery 2008; Smith 2008) are best understood when we consider the independent and inter-dependent effects of these systems of domination (see also Crenshaw 1991 and Smith 1998).

This race, class, and gender paradigm provides a framework for examining the data in this study for several reasons. First, as we will document, race, class, and gender shape both the risk and probability for experiencing and perpetrating IPV (gender differences) and the types of violence that are experienced (race and class variations). Second, because the race, class, and gender paradigm focuses on the ways in which power/privilege and oppression are organized by race, class, and gender, this model lends itself well to analyzing phenomenon — IPV — that feminists and other scholars agree are expressions of power and domination (Brownmiller 1975; Brush 2001; Brush, Raphael and Tolman 2003; Griffin 1979; Hattery 2008; Hattery and Kane 1995; Koss 1985, 1994; MacKinnon 1991; Renzetti 2001; Rich 1980, 1995). Thus, in this chapter, we utilize the race, class, and gender paradigm for examining and understanding the relationship between IPV and the variations in the racial composition of couples.

Figure 5-2 Racial Composition of the Couples

	Race of Male Partner		
	African American	White	Total
Race of Female Partner			
African American	308	11	319
White	43	441	484
Totals	381	452	

Experiences with IPV in Interracial Relationships: The Story

In order to carefully examine the role that the racial composition of the couples plays in rates of and risk for IPV, we must first break the issue down and look at each individual component separately. In other words, we must first examine the ways in which race shapes victimization and perpetration of IPV.

Race Differences in Victimization

Most, if not all, researchers who pay attention to rates of IPV across racial and ethnic lines note that IPV knows no boundaries. Women of all racial and ethnic groups are at risk for being the victims of IPV, "... domestic violence is statistically consistent across racial and ethnic boundaries" (Bureau of Justice Statistics Special Report: Violence Against Women: Estimates from the Redesigned Survey (NCJ-154348), August 1995, p. 3.) And, yet, when we analyzed the data from the National Violence Against Women (NVAW) survey (Tjaden and Thoennes 2000), we found that though the overall rates for experiencing IPV were the same, that African American women are more likely to report certain forms of IPV. Furthermore, the types of violence that African American women are more likely to experience are the more severe, near-lethal forms of IPV (Hattery & Smith 2003).

In summary, the data in Table 5-1 compare the percent of African American and White women who reported experiencing different forms of physical IPV during the last year. First, we should note that more than 25 percent of all women, regardless of race, report some type of physical IPV. The most common types of violence reported, regardless of race, are "being pushed, shoved or grabbed" by one's partner and "being slapped." Second, we should note that for half of the measures of physical IPV, there is no statistically significant difference between the experiences reported by African American and White women. However, for six of the most serious and lethal types of violence, African American women are *more likely* to report experiencing these forms of IPV than are White women. Specifically, African American women are 1.5 times more likely to report being "beat up" by their partners, "being threatened by a gun," or "having a knife used on them" by their intimate partners. Thus, we conclude that although race does not predict one's likelihood of experiencing IPV, race shapes the types of violence that victims experience.

Table 5-1 Rates of IPV by Race
(Percent of Women Reporting)

Types of Physical Violence	White	African American
Partner throws something at woman that could hurt her	10.1	9.3
Partner pushes, grabs, or shoves*	22.2	27.3
Partner pulls woman's hair	10.8	10.8
Partner slaps woman*	19.9	25.2
Partner kicks or bites woman*	6.2	8.6
Partner chokes or drowns woman	6.5	7.9
Partner hits woman with an object	6.8	7.9
Partner beats woman up*	9.8	14.7
Partner threatens woman with a gun*	4.9	7.7
Partner threatens woman with a knife	4.2	5.7
Partner uses a gun on woman	2.0	2.8
Partner uses a knife on woman*	2.2	3.8

* Race differences are significant at the $p < .1$ level.

Analyses were performed using the data collected as part of the Violence and Threats of Violence Against Women survey, a national probability sample of men and women. Descriptions and data can be found at: http://www.icpsr.umich.edu/cgi-bin/SDA.)

One of the strengths of quantitative survey data like that reported above is that it allows researchers to assess the prevalence of various types of violence among all Americans. One of the weaknesses, however, is that it does not always paint the picture of violence in a manner that is compelling to the reader. In contrast, stories generated by qualitative interviews are one of the strengths of this method. When we talk about the fact that African American women experience more severe, near lethal forms of violence, it often helps to hear the stories. When we began our interviews, we knew the statistics on violence and we knew that some of the women we would meet and interview would tell us of the horrors of IPV. Admittedly, we were struck by how common-place these stories were. Lara describes the night she was beaten up and hit in the head with a ball peen hammer.

> ... *he thought I had went somewhere. When he came here, I wasn't here, so I guess he thought I was out somewhere else. And he came in and we argued, and then, the push-ing started. He grabbed me and hit me with a hammer....* *right here. And like across my head, whatever ... They [her kids] heard it. They didn't see it, but they heard it, cause they were in the room. It was terrifying. So I went in the other room, locked myself in there, called the police and whatever, and they came. By that time, he was gone. And they came, and I was just hysterical, I mean, bleeding everywhere, and the kids screaming and hollering. And it was just a terrible night. It really was. And I went to the emergency room and I had to get maybe twelve or thirteen stitches, cause they were in different spots. I had like six up here, I had maybe three over here, and like maybe half on my ear. It was like hanging down, ripped off, so a plastic surgeon had to come in and sew it back up. I called her [a friend] and she came to my house and picked them [her kids] up. (Lara, twenty-something African American woman)*

In sum, the qualitative interviews we conducted complete the picture that the national data tell; namely that though violence, even severe violence, crosses all racial/ethnic lines, that African American women were more likely to report severe violence that required medical attention in the emergency room and even hos-pital stays. Furthermore, the analysis guided by the race, class, and gender paradigm reveals that race/ethnicity shapes women's expe-riences with victimization.

Race Differences in Perpetration

Next we examined the rates of physical IPV that men reported perpetrating. The data in Table 5-2 indicate a relatively high degree of consistency with the data reported by the women (Table 5-1). Approximately 25 percent of the men, regardless of race, report engaging in at least one act of physical IPV during the last twelve months, with the most common types of violence they report being "pushing, shoving or grabbing" their partners, "slapping" their partner, or "beating up" their partner. These are also the only types of physical IPV that African American men report perpetrating more frequently than their White counterparts.

Table 5-2 Rates of IPV by Race of Men Perpetrators (Percent of Men Reporting)

Types of Physical Violence	Race of Men	
	White	African American
Partner throws something at woman that could hurt her	8.8	10.0
Partner pushes, grabs, or shoves*	20.1	25.1
Partner pulls woman's hair	9.2	11.1
Partner slaps woman*	17.5	25.4
Partner kicks or bites woman	5.1	7.2
Partner chokes or drowns woman	5.3	6.8
Partner hits woman with an object	5.7	6.8
Partner beats woman up*	8.5	12.8
Partner threatens woman with a gun**	4.5	2.8
Partner threatens woman with a knife	3.8	4.8
Partner uses a gun on woman	1.8	1.4
Partner uses a knife on woman	2.0	2.8

* Race difference are significant at the p < .05 level.
** Race differences are significant at the p < .1 level.

Analyses were performed using the data collected as part of the Violence and Threats of Violence Against Women survey, a national probability sample of men and women. Descriptions and data can be found at: http://www.icpsr.umich.edu/cgi-bin/SDA.)

The fact that there are very few statistically significant differences in the rates of physical IPV perpetrated by African American and White men is especially important given the widespread beliefs among Whites that African American men are violent and dangerous (Davis 1983; Glassner 2000). In fact, the same basic trend holds on both sides of the IPV experience; just as there are few racial differences in the experiences women have as victims of IPV, there are few racial differences in the violence that men report perpetrating against their intimate partners.

Racial Composition of the Couple

In sum, there are few racial differences in either the perpetration or victimization experiences of physical IPV, yet those that do exist occur among the more dangerous, near-lethal forms of violence. When we consider these differences alongside the myth that African American men are more violent, and the concern many Americans continue to express about African American-White intimate relationships, we decided to examine rates of physical IPV in interracial couples and compare these to rates in intraracial (both African American and White) couples (Smith 2008).

African American Men and White Women

The data in Table 5-3 indicate the rates of physical IPV reported by women whose partners are African American men (the perpetrators).[5] In order to compare intra- and interracial rates of IPV, we include data for both African American women (intraracial)

---

5. Because of such a high rate of correlation between the reports of men and women we only analyzed the data reported by the women in the sample.

and White women (interracial). With the exception of "partner using a gun on woman," African American men are statistically significantly more likely to perpetrate every other type of physical IPV when their partners are White than when they are African American. Nearly half of all White women in relationships with African American men report they were "pushed, shoved, or grabbed." And, for most forms of physical IPV, White women are *more than twice as likely* to report at least one incident of violence than their African American counterparts. In other words, White women who are in relationships with African American men face a higher probability of experiencing physical IPV than African American women in relationships with African American men. Put another way, African American men are significantly more likely to engage in physical IPV when they are in interracial rather than intraracial relationships. (See Table 5-3.)

Table 5-3 Rates of IPV by African American Men by Race of Their Partner (Percent of Women Reporting)

Types of Physical Violence	Race of Victim	
	White (43)	African American (308)
Partner throws something at woman that could hurt her	25.6	7.8
Partner pushes, grabs, or shoves	46.5	22.1
Partner pulls woman's hair	32.6	8.1
Partner slaps woman	41.9	23.1
Partner kicks or bites woman	20.9	5.2
Partner chokes or drowns woman	18.6	5.2
Partner hits woman with an object	9.3	6.5
Partner beats woman up	25.6	11.0
Partner threatens woman with a gun	4.7	2.6
Partner threatens woman with a knife	11.6	3.9
Partner uses a gun on woman*	0.0	1.6
Partner uses a knife on woman	4.7	2.6

Race differences for all types of violence except (*) are significant at the p < .05 level.

Analyses were performed using the data collected as part of the Violence and Threats of Violence Against Women survey, a national probability sample of men and women. Descriptions and data can be found at: http://www.icpsr.umich.edu/cgi-bin/SDA.

White Men and African American Women

Finally, we turned to an examination of the likelihood of physical IPV occurring in relationships with White men. Again, this is based on the reports of African American and White women who are in relationships with White men (the perpetrators). The data in Table 5-4 indicate that African American women report almost no incidents of physical IPV when they are in relationships with White men. In contrast, the data for White women are nearly identical to the data reported in Table 5-2. Clearly, this high correlation in part reflects the fact that more than 97 percent of the White women who report physical IPV are in relationships with White men. Though the number of African American women in relationships with White men is very small, the data here suggest that African American women's probability for experiencing physical IPV is very, very low when they are in relationships with White men. Put another way, White men are *significantly less likely* to perpetrate physical IPV when they are in interracial relationships (with African American women) than when they are in intraracial relationships. (See Table 5-4.)

Race, Class and Gender: Analyzing the Data

The data presented in this chapter have demonstrated several important relationships. First, women's risk for experiencing physical IPV and men's likelihood of perpetrating physical IPV are *not* shaped by race. In other words, approximately 25 percent of women and 25 percent of men, regardless of race, report experiencing or perpetrating physical violence in their intimate partner relationships. However, as the data in Tables 5-1 and 5-2 demonstrate, race shapes the *types* of physical IPV that women experience and men perpetrate. Furthermore, we note that the role that race plays in shaping physical IPV is *stronger* for women than for men. African American women report significantly higher rates of near-lethal violence than do their White counterparts, whereas there are fewer

Table 5-4 Rates of IPV by White Men by Race of Their Partner (Percent of Women Reporting)

Types of Physical Violence	Race of Victim	
	White (441)	African American (11)
Partner throws something at woman that could hurt her	8.8	0
Partner pushes, grabs, or shoves	20.1	9.1
Partner pulls woman's hair	9.2	0
Partner slaps woman	17.5	0
Partner kicks or bites woman	17.5	9.1
Partner chokes or drowns woman	5.1	0
Partner hits woman with an object	5.3	0
Partner beats woman up	5.7	0
Partner threatens woman with a gun	8.5	0
Partner threatens woman with a knife	4.5	0
Partner uses a gun on woman	3.8	0
Partner uses a knife on woman	1.8	0

Race differences for all types of violence are significant at the $p < .05$ level.

Analyses were performed using the data collected as part of the Violence and Threats of Violence Against Women survey, a national probability sample of men and women. Descriptions and data can be found at: http://www.icpsr.umich.edu/cgi-bin/SDA.

significant differences in the types of violence that White and African American men report perpetrating.

However, when we examined physical IPV in interracial relationships — as compared to intraracial relationships — the results were highly significant and quite perplexing. In sum, African American men's probability for perpetrating violence is two to four times higher when they are in interracial relationships than when they are in intraracial relationships. In contrast, the reverse is true for White men; there were almost no instances of physical IPV reported in relationships between White men and African American women.

We turn to the race, class, and gender paradigm to explain this intriguing finding. We offer two possible explanations for this intriguing difference: (1) the access to institutional power that individuals in the couple have and (2) the perceptions outsiders have of the appropriateness of the union.

First, we suggest that when White men are in intimate relationships with African American women (a relatively rare interracial combination), the race and gender composition of the couple mirrors the race and gender hierarchies present in the U.S. (Zweigenhaft and Domhoff 2006) and thus, there is no reason for White men to use power and violence to assert dominance in their relationships. White men hold power imbued to them by patriarchy and White men hold power imbued to them by the system of racial domination in place in the U.S. (Baca Zinn and Thornton Dill 2005). Because the power in their intimate relationships is in line with the structures of societal power in which these relationships are embedded, White men in interracial relationships are more likely to feel comfortable with the gendered distribution of power in their relationships and therefore do not need to use violence to assert their masculinity and power over their female partners.

In contrast, when African American men and White women are in intimate relationships the result is a relationship that combines power and oppression in ways that may be inherently more egalitarian. African American men are imbued with power they draw from patriarchy, but this is balanced against the power that their White female partners draw from the system of racial domination. In these relationships, the power is balanced, overall, but it may seem out of balance with regards to the rigid gender roles Americans prescribe to intimate relationships dictating that men be the "head of the household" (Hattery 2001; Hochschild 1989; Kane 2006). For example, we ask, can an African American man be "head of the household" when he is in a relationship with a White woman who has access to racial power and privilege which may allow her to earn more money than he does?

Masculinity studies and studies of men who batter provide insight to unraveling this question (Smith 2008). Hegemonic masculinity is historically and culturally bound. Yet, according to Kimmel (2005) and Messner (2002), for most of the history of the United States, masculinity has been constructed around several key concepts: breadwinning, sexual prowess, and physical strength.[6]

When we consider the issue of breadwinning, for example, it is important to note that unemployment, a common experience for African American men, throws off the gendered pattern of wage earning in intimate partnerships (Smith 2008). Furthermore, men who batter report that they beat their partners specifically as a show of masculinity in order to re-establish the gender roles dictated by hegemonic masculinity, femininity and heterosexuality (Hattery & Smith 2007; Hattery 2008; Smith 2008). There are many ways for a man to assert his masculinity, thus one might ask, why does he engage in violence? Simply put, because an act of physical IPV—a demonstration of physical power—may be interpreted as the most potent demonstration of one's masculine identity. Furthermore, because the victim of this violence (physical or sexual), his female partner, is the very being who is the *perceived cause* of the power imbalance—because she appears to have power that she is not entitled to—the man is able to vindicate his masculinity through a single act of violence. Furthermore, his act of violence creates a power vacuum that restores the balance of power to the gendered state in which it "should be" under a system of patriarchal oppression.

What is particularly interesting about the use of violence to create and reinforce power is that the batterer believes that his female partner is the cause of the power imbalance, when as sociologists we note that it is the inequality regimes of patriarchy and racial superiority (Acker 2006) that create power and inequality in the first place. And, it is the particular configuration of these inequality regimes in interracial relationships between African American men and White women that creates the egalitarianism that violates the gendered "marital" contract. Ironically, it is the state of egalitarianism itself—which might seem to provide protection from IPV—that

---

6. Furthermore, this construct of masculinity is so pervasive that is socialized early on. For example, Kane (2006) documents, using qualitative interviews, the mechanism by which parents teach their children "gender" and notes that fathers in particular are quick to "discipline" their sons when they behave in "non-masculine" ways.

can be perceived as a threat to African American men's sense of manhood and power which in turn can provide a "trigger" for IPV (see Hattery & Smith 2007; Hattery 2008; Smith 2008).

A second possible "trigger" to IPV may be found in the dissatisfaction, disapproval, resentment, and even violence that is expressed toward interracial couples. We note that of all interracial relationship, it is those between African American men and White women that cause Americans the most discomfort and which are the most likely to draw violence from the outside.[7] Perhaps the resentment that is expressed to and experienced by African American men who choose to be in committed relationships with White women is somehow turned by these men on their female partners. Much like the example of the "breadwinner," this might be yet another example of the ways in which men, in this case African American men, respond to antagonism against a misidentified "offending party:" the women they choose to partner with, rather than toward the real source of the antagonism: disapproving outsiders. This phenomenon is similar to the oft invoked belief that men come home frustrated with their boss and kick the dog. Thus, we suggest that more research on interracial relationships focus on the dialectic between "inside" and "outside" violence.

Conclusion

In this chapter, we have examined the ways in which the racial/ethnic composition of a couple shapes the likelihood of IPV and the types of IPV that are most likely to be experienced. Analysis of nationally representative data indicates that IPV is significantly shaped by the racial/ethnic composition of the couple. Specifically, African American men are significantly more likely to engage in physical IPV when their partners are White than when their

---

7. We note that "relationships" — often non-consensual — between White men and African American women were common during slavery and Jim Crow and were an accepted part of White male privilege.

partners are African American women. In contrast, White men are significantly less likely to engage in physical IPV when their partners are African American than when their partners are White women. Thus, African American-White interracial relationships are more violent than intraracial relationships *only* when the male partner is African American; in contrast, White men are more prone to violence in intra, rather than inter-racial relationships.

Myths about the violent tendencies of African American men (Davis 1983; Hill-Collins 2004; Hill 2005; Smith 2008, hooks 2004) would have us conclude that the problem is that African American men are just more violent than White men. Yet, these data, specifically the data in Table 5-2 (men's perpetration of IPV), indicate that White and African American men are equally violent, but that their rates of engaging in physical IPV are shaped by the race of their intimate partners. This finding alone moves us beyond the simplistic analysis that relies on the old assumptions of African American male violent behavior. The second finding, that White men are significantly less violent in interracial relationships raises several important questions about the appropriate explanation. Because this cell is so small and these relationships are so rare, its possible that the findings reflected here are a result of a statistical artifact—the small cell size for White male-African American female relationships—and/or a selection factor, specifically that there is something "different" about the White men who choose to enter into relationships with African American women. Yet, neither of these explanations undermines the theoretical argument made in this chapter, which remains supported even when limiting the discussion to the statistically significant finding for African American men who perpetrate physical IPV. These findings thus force scholars to analyze the roles that race, gender and couple composition play in the complexities of IPV.

Utilizing the race, class, and gender paradigm as a lens through which to interpret these findings we argue that systems of race and gender domination and oppression are experienced and "performed"[8] in individual relationships and that one expression of this is IPV. We argued that understanding these systems of race and gender domination and oppression help us to explain the ways in which IPV is shaped by race and gender as well as by the racial/ethnic composition of the couple. These findings have policy implications. Specifically we suggest that in order to design successful prevention and intervention programs these must be tailored not only to the race of the victims and the offenders but also the racial/ethnic composition of the couple.

Bibliography

Acker, Joan. 2006. *Class Questions, Feminist Answers*. New York: Routledge.

Anderson, M. L. 2001. "Restructuring for Whom? Race, Class, Gender, and the Ideology of Invisibility." *Sociological Forum* 16:181–201.

Baca Zinn, M. and B. Thornton Dill. 2000. "Theorizing Difference from Multiracial Feminism." In *Gender Through the Prism of Difference*. Maxine Baca Zinn, Pierrette Hodnagneu-Sotelo, and Michael Messner (eds). Needham Heights, MA: Allyn and Bacon.

Bonilla-Silva, Eduardo and Tyrone Forman. 2000. "I am Not A Racist But." *Discourse and Society*, 11:50–85.

Brownmiller, Susan. 1975. *Against Our Will, Men, Women, and Rape*. New York: Bantam Books.

Brush, Lisa. D. 2001. "Poverty, Battering, Race, and Welfare Reform: Black-White Differences in Women's Welfare-to-Work Transitions." *Journal of Poverty*, 5, 67–89.

Brush, L. D., Raphael, Jody, and Tolman, Richard. 2003. "Effects of Work on Hitting and Hurting." *Violence against Women*, 9(10), 1213–1230.

---

8. See West and Zimmerman's concept of "doing gender" West, Candace and Don H. Zimmerman. 1987. "Doing Gender." *Gender and Society* 1:125–151.

Collins, Patricia Hill. 2004. *Black Sexual Politics: African Americans, Gender, and the New Racism*. New York: Routledge Publishers.

Crenshaw, K. 1991. "Mapping the Margins: Intersectionality, Identity Politics, and Violence against Women of Color." *Stanford Law Review*, 43, (6) 1241–1299.

Davis, Angela. 1983. *Women, Race, and Class*. New York: Vintage Books.

Esqueda, C. 2005. "The influence of gender role stereotypes, the woman's race, and level of provocation and resistance on domestic violence culpability attributions." *Sex Roles: A Journal of Research*.

Griffin, Susan. 1979. *Rape: The Politics of Consciousness*. New York: Harper & Row.

Hattery, A.J. 2001. "Tag-Team Parenting: Costs and benefits of utilizing non-overlapping shift work patterns in families with young children." *Families in Society*, *82*(4), 419–427.

Hattery, Angela. 2008. *Intimate Partner Violence*. New York: Rowman & Littlefield.

Hattery, Angela and Earl Smith. 2008. "Incarceration: A Tool for Racial Segregation and Labor Exploitation." *Race, Gender and Class*. 15(1/2): 79–98.

Hattery, Angela and Earl Smith. 2007. *African American Families*. California: SAGE.

Hattery, Angela. 2001. *Women, work, and family: balancing and weaving*. Thousand Oaks, Calif.: Sage Publications.

Hattery, Angela J. and Kane, Emily W. 1995. "Men's and Women's Perceptions of Non-Consensual Sexual Intercourse." *Sex Roles* 33:785–802.

Hill, S.A. and Sprague, J. 1999. "Parenting in Black and White Families: The Interaction of Gender with Race and Class." *Gender and Society*, 13 (4):480–502.

Hill, Shirley. 2005. *Black Intimacies: A Gender Perspective on Families and Relationships : A Gender Perspective on Families and Relationships*. Lanham, MD: Altamira Press.

Hill-Collins, Patricia. 1994. "Shifting the Center: Race, Class, and Feminist Theorizing About Motherhood." Pp. 45–66 in E. Glenn. G. Chang and L. Forcey (ed.), *Mothering: Ideology, Experience, and Agency.* New York: Routledge.

Hochschild, Arlie Russel. 1989. *The Second Shift.* New York: Penguin Books.

hooks, bell. 2004. *We Real Cool: Black Men and Masculinity.* New York: Routledge.

Johnson, James H. 1970. *Race Relations in Virginia & Miscegenation in the South, 1776–1860.* Amherst, Massachusetts: University of Massachusetts Press.

Kane, Emily. 2006. "No Way My Boys Are Going to Be Like That: Parents' Responses to Children's Gender Nonconformity." *Gender & Society.* 20:149–176.

Kimmel, Michael. 2005. *Manhood in America.* New Edition. New York: Oxford University Press.

King, D. 1988. "Multiple Jeopardy, Multiple Consciousness: The Context of a Black Feminist Ideology." *Signs.* 14(1).

Koss, Mary.P. 1985. "The hidden rape victim: Personality, attitudinal, and situational characteristics." *Psychology of Women Quarterly.* 9:193–212.

MacKinnon, Catharine. 1991. *Toward a Feminist Theory of the State.* Cambridge, MA: Harvard University Press.

Messner, Michael. 2002. *Taking the Field: Women, Men, and Sports.* Minnesota: University of Minnesota Press.

Padavic, Irene and Barbara F. Reskin. 2002. *Women and Men at Work.* Thousand Oaks: Pine Forge Press.

Qian, Zhenchao. 2005. "Breaking the Last Taboo: Interracial Marriage in America." *Contexts* 4:33–37.

Rennison, Callie Marie. 2003. "Intimate Partner Violence, 1993–2001." United States Department of Justice, Bureau of Justice Statistics, Washington, DC.

Renzetti, Claire M. 2001. "One Strike and You're Out: Implications of a Federal Crime Control Policy for Battered Women." *Violence against Women,* 7(6), 685–698.

Rich, Adrienne. 1995. *Of Woman Born: Motherhood as Experience and Institution.* New York: W.W. Norton and Company.

Rich, Adrienne. 1980. "Compulsory Heterosexuality and Lesbian Existence." *Signs.* 5:631–660.

Simmons, Tavia & O'Connell, Martin. 2003. *Married-Couple and Unmarried-Partner Households: 2000 Census 2000 Special Reports.* Washington, DC: U.S. Bureau of the Census.

Smith, Earl. 2008. African American Men and Intimate Partner Violence. Journal of African American Studies. 12:156–179.

Smith, V. 1998. *Not Just Race, Not Just Gender: Black Feminist Readings.* London: Routledge Publishing.

Tjaden, Patricia, and Nancy Thoennes. *Violence and Threats of Violence Against Women and Men in the United States, 1994–1996* [Computer file]. ICPSR02566-v1. Denver, CO: Center for Policy Research [producer], 1998. Ann Arbor, MI: Inter-university Consortium for Political and Social Research [distributor], 1999.

U.S. Bureau of the Census. 1972. *U.S. Census of Population: 1970,* vol. 1. Washington, DC: Government Printing Office.

U.S. Bureau of the Census.1999. *Race of Wife by Race of Husband: 1999.* Washington, DC. Government Printing Office.

West, Candace and Don H. Zimmerman. 1987. "Doing Gender." *Gender and Society* 1:125–151.

Western, B. 2006. *Punishment and Inequality in America.* New York: Russell Sage.

Zinn, Baca and B. Thornton Dill. 2005. "Theorizing Differences from Multicultural Feminism." Pp. 23–28 in *Gender Through the Prism of Difference,* edited by M. B. Zinn, P. Hondagneu-Sotelo, and M. A. Messner: Oxford University Press.

Zweigenhaft, Richard and G. William Domhoff. 2006. *Diversity in the Power Elite.* New York: Rowman and Littlefield.

Chapter 6

Hiding in Plain Sight: Why Queer Interraciality Is Unrecognizable to Strangers and Sociologists

Amy C. Steinbugler

In the past several decades, interracial intimacy has been a central lens through which sociologists have examined racial power, stratification, and the maintenance of racial and ethnic boundaries—particularly those between Blacks and Whites. This line of research has demonstrated the complex cultural strategies involved when interracial couples traverse public and intimate spaces, suggesting the significance of social, spatial, and symbolic boundaries to the formation of Black-White interracial families (Drake and Cayton 1945). More recently, qualitative research has explored the racial subtext of everyday interraciality in the post-Civil Rights Era, uncovering important continuities and divergences from earlier decades (Childs 2005; Dalmage 2000; McNamara et al. 1999; Rosenblatt et al. 1995). Though interracial partners are less likely to face overt racial violence, they still encounter many challenges, including racially segregated neighborhoods and social spaces, resistance from families, and identity formation with children (this topic is explored in chapter 4). Because scholarship on interracial intimacy has focused almost exclusively on heterosexual interracial couples, it has failed to critically analyze how racial difference is experienced in lesbian and gay relationships. Further, researchers have neglected to problematize heterosexuality itself, overlooking the ways in which heterosexuality shapes interracial identities, relationships, and interactions. My aim is to open up a wider lens on the subject of interracial intimacy by introducing sexual identity as a critical influence (Steinbugler 2005; 2007).[1] In this essay I draw upon in-depth interviews and ethnographic observation to examine how sexuality and gender influence the everyday experiences of lesbian, gay, and heterosexual couples by focusing on the issue of social recognition in public spaces.[2]

I begin by discussing the relevance of social recognition, or visibility, to studies of sexuality, and offer this as a useful framework for thinking about public experiences of interracial intimacy. I then describe types of public interactions through which heterosexual couples experience social recognition, contrasting these with the more profound invisibility than many gay and lesbian partners experience in public spaces. Lastly, I show how heterosexuality privileges interracial couples, even as it makes them vulnerable to harassment, suggesting a more dynamic quality to this sexual status than is generally understood.

---

1. In this essay I alternate using terms gay/lesbian and queer, though I do not mean to indicate with this practice that they are interchangeable. "Queer" is a more expansive term in that it acknowledges the fluidity of gender and sexual identities and destabilizes the hetero/homo binary, but it may also be overly narrow in its emergence at a relatively recent political historical moment—the early 1990s. Younger respondents in this study were more likely than older respondent to claim this identity. Here I describe each partner's sexuality with the terms they use themselves and when speaking more broadly I alternate between them.

2. In earlier writing (see Steinbugler 2005) I have primarily utilized the concepts of "visibility" and "invisibility" to discuss the ways in which interracial intimacy is recognized or goes unseen in public places. However, using the term "invisible" to describe lesbian and gay intimacy may obscure a range of social class, race, and gender privileges that individual partners experience, even as they inhabit a marginalized sexual status. In this essay I therefore move towards conceptualizing the perception of being seen or unseen as a form of social recognition, a term that signals more pointedly the recognition of intimacy between partners and not the visibility of individual subjects.

Sexuality, Interracial Intimacy, and Social Recognition

In this essay, I foreground the sexual status of Black/White interracial couples by focusing on the issue of social recognition, or visibility. I depart from previous analyses by examining lesbian, gay, and heterosexual interracial narratives, using this broader lens to more fully capture the complex social relations that influence public experiences of interraciality. Guided by feminist theories of intersectionality (Crenshaw 1991; Baca Zinn and Thornton Dill 1996; Collins 1991), my aim is to move beyond transgressing the "color line" as a one-dimensional metaphor for theorizing interracial intimacy, towards a more complex analysis that acknowledges structures of gender and heteronormativity.

The concept of visibility has been theorized largely in relation to sexual identities and structures. Within a dominant heterosexual paradigm, presumptions of heterosexuality infuse our social world. Inhabiting a naturalized and normative status, heterosexual identities and social spaces are simultaneously visible in their ubiquity and seemingly invisible in their naturalness — they are 'invisibly visible' (Brickell, 2000). In this way, heterosexual intimacy receives social recognition both *formally*, through laws and social policies that reward heterosexuality, and *informally* through everyday acknowledgement and affirmation of heterosexuality as normative. Because heterosexuals, lesbians, and gays are diverse social groups, privileges of heterosexuality are modified by cross-cutting statuses, including social class, race, and gender (Cohen 1997).

In contrast, gays and lesbians have historically struggled for greater visibility through social movements and activism (D'Emilio and Freedman 1988). They have also fought for a place within social and critical theory (Cohen 1997; Fogg-Davis 2006; Smith 1998). Recently, media scholars have proclaimed a surge in U.S. lesbian and gay visibility, including "out" television stars; "out" sports stars and rock stars; and gay days at family theme parks (Dow 2001; Walters 2001). Yet, these representations reflect a particular demographic: mostly male, mostly White, and mostly upper-middle class

(Gross 2001). Furthermore, the increased circulation of glossy images of queer bodies does not necessarily translate into greater social recognition or safety for actual queer bodies that walk through city streets and interact with strangers. This is especially true for queers of color (Hernandez 2004; Wright 2008).

The micro-politics of public interaction have also received sustained attention from qualitative studies of interracial intimacy. Since Drake and Cayton's (1945) classical study of Black neighborhoods on Chicago's South Side, a growing number of scholars have undertaken qualitative and ethnographic research that investigates the spatial and symbolic boundaries that challenge the formation of [heterosexual] Black-White interracial intimacy (Childs 2005; Dalmage 2000; Frankenberg 1993; McNamara et al. 1999; Porterfield 1978; Rosenblatt et al. 1995).[3] These scholars have illustrated the variety of ways in which [heterosexual] Black-White couples receive attention from unknown others in public places — through stares, comments, questions, and sometimes verbal or even physical harassment. They also argue that in other instances, interracial couples and families can feel unrecognized or unseen (Childs 2005; Dalmage 2000; Twine and Steinbugler 2006).

While this phenomenon of feeling alternately conspicuous and inconspicuous in public spaces could be aptly understood through a framework of visible and invisible sexualities, studies of interracial intimacy are not generally framed in this manner. The sexual identities of interracial partners are rarely examined (but see Frankenberg 1993). While studies of interraciality have focused almost exclusively on heterosexual couples, they have not examined how heterosexuality impacts the identities, relationships, and public interactions of interracial partners. In this way, heterosexuality is normalized and these couples — though they have been historically stereotyped as sexual deviants — are not seen as possessing a notable sexual identity, just like Whites are often not seen as pos-

---

3. I bracket heterosexuality when research is exclusively but implicitly heterosexualized — when data is derived exclusively from heterosexual narratives without explicitly discussing how heterosexuality shaped those narratives.

sessing a particular racial identity.[4] Further, conceptualizing inter-racial intimacy through the lens of sexuality brings into focus the experience of lesbian and gay partners. In this essay, I use this lens to examine how sexuality affects the ways in which interracial part-ners experience visibility or invisibility in public spaces.

Research Methodology

Qualitative data for this analysis are drawn from a non-random, snowball sample of lesbian, gay, and heterosexual Black/White cou-ples in the metropolitan areas of New York City, Philadelphia, and Washington D.C. The sample includes eighty in-depth, semi-struc-tured interviews conducted with forty Black/White couples in 2005–2006. These couples varied in gender and sexuality such that twenty couples are heterosexual and twenty are same-sex. Of the het-erosexual couples, ten involve a Black man and White woman, and ten involve a Black woman and White man. Of the same-sex cou-ples, ten are lesbian and ten are gay. This project takes Black/White couples as its focus because the color line between Blacks and Whites in the United States has been one of the most fiercely and violently contested, creating a unique set of social and cultural meanings around Black/White interraciality.

In conducting this study, I utilized a snowball sampling tech-nique to make contact with additional respondents who were in the extended social networks of original interviewees. Unlike other re-searchers in this area, I interviewed each partner in every couple separately. Interviews usually took place in the respondents' home, ranged from 45 to 150 minutes in length, and were audio-taped and transcribed in their entirety.[5] In addition, to examine how interra-

---

4. Because heterosexual interracial couples have long been read as sex-ually perverse, interracial partners and the sociologists who study them may be especially wary of examining interraciality as a sexual status.

5. The author, a queer White woman, conducted 75 of the interviews and 5 were conducted by a research assistant, who is a queer Black man. The research assistant interviewed four gay Black men and one hetero-

ciality is constructed through social interaction, qualitative interviews were augmented by participant observation with four couples from the sample. During these observations I shadowed partners in numerous social spaces, including libraries, high-school football games, Parent Teacher Association meetings, neighborhood parks, kitchens and living rooms. I conducted at least 18 visits with each of the four couples over a period of approximately six weeks.

Seeing Straight: Heterosexual Interracial Intimacy in Public Spaces

Exclusion and Affirmation

Qualitative research has shown that heterosexual Black/White couples experience the stares, long looks, side comments and threats of physical violence that come with embodying a long-restricted and heavily-surveilled sexual status—Black/White interracial sexuality (Childs 2005, Dalmage 2000, Rosenblatt et al. 1995). Heterosexual partners in this study experienced these same forms of social exclusion—subtle and not so subtle reminders in shopping malls, restaurants, and city streets that their relationships violate monoracial sexual norms. Though Philadelphia, New York, and Washington D.C. represent three of the most racially diverse urban areas in the nation, the racial segregation that structures their residential neighborhoods is mapped onto intimate bodies. The heterosexual interracial partners I interviewed felt the attention—whether it was curious, hostile, or affirmative—of strangers in public spaces.

Feeling conspicuous in public reinforces to heterosexual couples that their interraciality is a public identity. It is a symbol from which strangers draw a host of social, cultural, or historic meanings. Interracial partners may not always be able to discern *how* strangers read their intimacy, but they often know that something about their racial and gender difference intrigues, offends, or confuses others.

---

sexual Black man. There are not significant differences in substance or depth between these interviews and those conducted by the author.

Christopher Tomlinson, a heterosexual African-American man whose relationship with his White partner, Lana Keyes, has strained many of his close friendships, explains how he interprets others' reactions:

> In relationship to my outlook or perception in society, it's weakened my thought process of America in relationship to race and acceptance … Most statistics say that Black and White people in interracial relationships are accepted. But in reality, my whole experience has been wild, because the whole accepting thing is an issue on all levels, not just stereotyping [or] the KKK. It's the everyday focus — people's actions or attitudes, no matter how subtle.

The intense and persistent attention Christopher receives in public spaces reflects the hypervisibility of relationships between Black men and White women. Other interracial partners echoed Christopher's observation. Myron Tanner, a fifty-year old Black man, explains that he often feels conspicuous when he's out with his White wife because as a pair they're easily noticed. "It comes up all the time. I mean, there's a striking contrast between Nancy and I, you know? I'm taller than her. She's short. I'm Black. [She's] White and blond … I'm always conscious about that." These relationships may be more recognizable in part because they are a larger demographic group — 75 percent of all Black/White marriages are between Black men and White women (U.S. Census 2000). Their hypervisibility may also derive from the symbolic power of this historical archetype as an invocation of the myth of the Black rapist and White anxieties over racial purity and "social equality" (Hodes 1997; Higginbotham 1978; Drake and Cayton 1945; Romano 2003).

These narratives also suggest that gender influences how interracial partners are perceived in public. Relationships between Black men and White women are the most visible of all Black/White relationships; they elicited outwardly vocal and threatening reactions from Whites. For Black women and White men in romantic relationships, there is more variation in the type of recognition they experience in public spaces. The connection between these partners is sometimes overtly recognized, as when Black women are verbally harassed by Black men on city streets while in the company of their White male partner. At other times, they perceive their intimacy to be unrecognizable.

Heterosexual partners in this study also experienced social recognition that was ostensibly positive. These encounters reflect the popularity in some communities of a multiracial ethic in which interracial intimacy is assumed to embody the potential for racial transformation. From this perspective, interraciality represents "love's revolution" (Root 2001). In these interactions, interraciality is read not as deviant or disruptive, but as progressive and righteous, a promise of a more cohesive racial future. Ethan Smolen, a twenty-nine-year-old White heterosexual man, relays the variety of public reactions he and his Black partner, Wanda Maurillo, receive in their Philadelphia neighborhood and its surrounding environs.

> People are screwy. You had the people that would see Wanda wearing dreadlocks walking down the streets with a White man and have to make a comment about her being a traitor. Or you would have even more frustrating—or not frustrating but annoying—would be the people that would be like, "It's so good what you're doing." Like we're doing a community service project to promote racial harmony. "Oh that's good. That must be so hard here in America."

Ethan's observation and those of many heterosexual partners in my study make clear that whether the reaction that he and his partner elicit from strangers is antagonistic or affirmative, their intimacy carries a comprehensible social meaning. Bradley Tyson, a heterosexual Black husband, makes a similar assessment when I ask him whether he and his White wife, Julianna Tyson, receive looks or stares in public spaces. He says, "Yeah, we do ... And we know it. But I don't think those looks are all hostile looks. They're just curious or congratulations. [They] go, 'Wish we saw more people like that.'" Bradley and Julianna, like Ethan and Wanda, are read as intimate partners, with all the rewards or baggage that this brings. As heterosexual couples, they inhabit a sexual status that—

whether or not it is deemed problematic—is legible to others. Their stories demonstrate that heterosexual interraciality is a meaningful social category from which strangers make various types of judgments and assumptions.

Heterosexuality as Visual Default

Black/White interracial narratives illustrate how presumptions of heterosexuality structure public spaces. Sexuality scholars have explored the powerful ways in which heterosexuality configures social life—what kinds of desire, intimacy, behavior, and family are considered normative and natural (Evans 1993). Drawing on Monique Wittig, Warner argues that "Western political thought has taken the heterosexual couple to represent the principle of social union itself" (1993: xxi). Many heterosexual partners I interviewed, especially Black men and White women, were confident that their intimacy was visible and comprehensible to the strangers they encountered in their daily lives. They experience their intimacy as an obvious and unremarkable fact and did not believe that physical contact was necessary to convey their intimacy to others. When I ask Julianna, a thirty-four-year-old White heterosexual woman and mother of nine-year-old Violet whether she believes people recognize her and Bradley as a couple, her answer and her incredulous tone suggest that she finds my question somewhat absurd. "Yeah! I think so. I mean we don't walk around like I am over there and he is somewhere trailing behind. We are next to one another, you know? So it's not like we have to hold hands."

These narratives further suggest that for heterosexual interracial partners—especially Black men and White women—racial difference may actually heighten presumptions of heterosexual intimacy. The archetypal figure of racial/sexual deviance, a Black man with a White woman is such a powerful and evocative image that others may read this historic symbol onto two individuals who are simply occupying the same physical space. Kalvin Oster, a thirty-year-old heterosexual Black man, explains how racial and gender differences are coded as interracial sexuality even in the absence of physical contact. Growing up in a small Delaware city, Kalvin was

once attacked at a stop-light after school while in the car with a
young White female friend. A White man driving a pick-up truck
with a gun-rack pulled up alongside their car at the intersection. Kalvin
describes what followed:

> He starts yelling racial slurs at her and she was just a
> friend. I wasn't even dating her. He was saying, "You
> nigger lover!" and spitting out the window, and then
> get outs the truck and starts grabbing on the door. It
> was ridiculous.

In this instance heterosexual intimacy is mapped onto a Black young
man and a White young woman simply because they are sitting together in the same car at a stoplight.

Shawn Tarwick, a 49-year old White gay man, also explains that
he gets negative attention on city streets at lunchtime while he is walking with a female African American coworker. "I've had African
American men say nasty things to me. You know, 'What are you
doing with her?'" The intensity of the harassment in these two examples is clearly different—the White man in the pickup truck
began to physically assault the car Kalvin sat in while the African
American men on the street verbally derided Shawn. Yet what is
noticeably similar about these two accounts is the way in which
two friends—a woman and a man—are assumed to be romantic
partners by the simple fact of sharing physical space. In other words,
what would two people of different races and different genders be
doing together if they were not involved in some sort of sexual relationship? The reality of racial segregation may render heterosexual intimacy the default assumption.

Queer Interraciality: Intimacy Unseen

The Privileges and Vulnerability of Social Recognition

While gay and lesbian interracial partners do not always experience the same levels of visibility in public spaces, their narratives
are qualitatively different from the stories told by many heterosexual interracial partners. Though gender shapes how individuals in

heterosexual Black/White couples feel themselves perceived in restaurants, stores, and on city streets, for many, public experiences are marked by expressions of social recognition. Their intimacy is visible to unknown others. Whether this recognition registers as affirmation, curiosity or hostility, straight interracial couples bear the marker of interraciality as a cultural symbol—with all of the historical, social, and political meanings it carries. In contrast, many of the gay and lesbian partners in this study perceived their intimacy to be unrecognizable in most public spaces and did not interpret their interraciality as having a public identity whatsoever. Some partners expressed this observation as a conviction that "gay trumps interracial." To be marked as interracial requires first that two individuals are understood to be intimates, and many queer couples felt that their sexuality precluded this understanding. Or if their intimacy was made visible through public displays of affection, some partners felt it was their sexuality and not their interraciality that made them vulnerable to harassment or physical attack. Their sexuality, in other words, did not aggravate their racial difference, or imbue it with social meaning. Only in spaces that were self-consciously marked as lesbian, gay, or queer did they perceive their interraciality to be recognizable or meaningful.

Many queer interracial partners (especially women), experience a profound sense that their relationship is invisible to others in public spaces. This assessment derives from numerous quotidian experiences, such as having supermarket clerks separate their groceries, waiters and waitresses offer to seat them separately, or being hit on by a stranger even while their partner stands beside them. Maureen Wiley, a thirty-year-old White woman who lives in Washington D.C. with her Black partner, Terrina Nissar, describes a typical occurrence:

> We have this thing that we always laugh about. We'll be in a crowded space—like a bus or a movie—[and] people always cut in between us. Cause if you see a couple, you don't cut in between them. You know what I mean? But people just cut right in between us ... I think [Terrina] gets more annoyed at it. I think it's hysterical. I'm like, "Hello? Together." Um, I'm sure I've cut off people

that I haven't seen were together either whether they're together intimately or just together hanging out. I have my own assumptions of who knows who.

Though they interpret it differently, the repetitive nature of this type of experience reinforces a shared sense that they inhabit a marginal intimacy that is unrecognizable to others.

Many queer interracial couples believe that in public spaces—unless they are physically touching—they often pass as friends. Dionna Yates, a 23-year old Black lesbian who grew up in North Carolina and now lives in Philadelphia, explains this perspective:

> [On] a continuum of things that made my life hard, being in an interracial relationship would be on the lower end of the continuum than like being a Black person. 'Cause like not a lot of people see that. In public people don't even perceive us as a couple. They see two friends hanging out or whatever.

In contrast to her Blackness, which is always visible, Deidre's interracial relationship is almost never visible. Writing on the "politics of passing," Carol Johnson (2002) argues that same-sex bodies not touching in public is admittedly a strange form of passing as heterosexual, but that this performance of heterosexuality is precisely what is often expected or required of lesbian and gay couples in public spaces. Queer couples often pass as heterosexual friends, not same-sex lovers.

Lesbian and gay interracial partners become more visible by holding hands or being physically affectionate in public spaces. Public displays of affection (PDAs) also make queer partners more vulnerable to harassment or physical violence, creating a particular paradox around visible sexualities (see Steinbugler 2005). For queer interracial couples, social recognition often comes at a price. To negotiate the privileges and perils of social recognition queer partners manage visibility through conscious decisions about where and how to express affection (Lasser and Tharinger 2003). Some partners are reluctant to show affection in any social setting they do not recognize as gay/lesbian or queer, such as bars, clubs, restaurants, or particular city blocks or neighborhoods. Others adamantly would not censor or modify their behavior in public to suit the prejudices or preferences of strangers. Partners with this outlook willingly endured curious or hostile stares. Both of these approaches acknowledge that refraining from public displays of affection permits the possibility of passing as heterosexual friends.[6]

When gay and lesbian interracial partners kiss, hold hands, or show affection in public spaces, these effusive acts reflect feelings of intimacy and love, as they do for heterosexuals. However, structures of heterosexism and homophobic attitudes put these acts in a different social context. Queer partners out themselves with every overtly intimate gesture. Because queer affection is starkly visible against presumptions of heterosexual intimacy, some partners engage in public displays of affection to assert or "perform" intimacy. In *Weaving a Family*, Barbara Katz Rothman explains that as a White mother she consciously performs small acts and gestures through which she attempts to make her connection to her adopted Black daughter obvious. As Rothman "does" family, so too do some queer interracial partners make conscious decisions to "do" intimacy.

Tommy Smith-Donnell, a gay Black man with big round glasses and a warm, gregarious personality, and his White partner, Brian Smith-Donnell, possessed a unique strategy towards disrupting the invisibility that often characterized queer intimacy. Tommy and Brian have been together for twelve years and live in a racially mixed working-class community in Philadelphia. When I meet Tommy, he is wearing dark blue jeans, a sunny yellow long-sleeve cotton shirt, brown leather loafers and a small round black pin with the words "Erase Racism" scrawled in white letters. Upon meeting Brian that same day I immediately notice his attire because he is wearing the *exact* same outfit-dark blue jeans, yellow long-sleeve shirt and brown loafers with an "Erase Racism" pin. The image of two men over fifty dressed in identical clothing is striking. Tommy explains that

---

6. This notion of passing is specific to a North American culture in which female friends typically don't hold hands in public, but might sometimes walk arm-in-arm and male friends generally do neither. This norm shifts in other parts of the world.

this is precisely why they've been dressing the same for the past twelve years, to demand social recognition:

> We do everything a straight couple can do—hold hands, kiss in public, be close, laugh, whatever! Wear each other clothes ... That's one reason why we dress alike ... Everywhere we go we'll dress alike. It proves, it proves the point ... It says to society that this is possible. "You say it's impossible, it *is* possible." There's a lot of people around here who [are] together and don't dress alike, but they're still together, okay? We're, we're speaking for them too, in our own little way ... We're not gonna wear a sign, we don't have to hit you in your face about it. We're just there, you know. To prove the point.

Tommy and Brian's decision to counter invisibility by dressing identically is a unique response to a common perception among lesbian and gay men in this study—that they are rarely read as a couple in public spaces. As a result, Tommy and Brian likely experience the greatest level of visibility of any gay or lesbian partners I interviewed—it is impossible not to notice that they go together. This pronounced visibility is the result of an elaborate appeal for social recognition.

Some same-sex partners in the study were surprised when others did not recognize them as a couple. Their surprise originated from an assumption that people would recognize intimacy in their comfortable exchanges or in the closeness of the space that they shared. This expectation more closely characterized the experiences of gay men in my study, some of whom were confident that "you can just tell" they are a couple. Kirk Belton-Davis, a forty-four-year-old gay White man who has been with his Black partner, Walter Belton-Davis, for twenty-four years explains his own assumptions:

> I think most people probably figure it out because we are very much like a couple. How we talk here is how we talk everywhere. I think it's fairly obvious, but some people are fairly dense.

In this study, lesbians made the most claims to invisibility. This may reflect their social location — the joint workings of sexism, racism, and heteronormativity privilege certain bodies and marginalize others. Some interracial partners suggested that gay intimacy generally may be more visible than lesbian intimacy because interracial pairs or groups of women are more likely to be read as friends, while a Black man and a White man are unlikely to be socializing on a city street or in a restaurant unless they are doing business.[7] Victor Renford, a fifty-year-old gay White man, argued that examples of Black men and White men together are so scarce that people don't know how to place it. Describing an experience he had while working in a social service agency, he says, "I was with a Black man going to make a home call and they thought we were the police because that's when they saw Black and White men together."

Visibility and the Performance of Gender

Gender presentation affected the visibility of interracial intimacy for many of the lesbian partners in my study. Lesbians are often stereotyped as transgressors of traditional femininity — short-haired, aggressive, androgynous women who flout social conventions and only wear pants. When lesbians express a gender identity that falls outside of this rigid prescription, or when very feminine-looking lesbians move through non-queer public spaces without their female partner, they are assumed to be heterosexual — the default sexual identity. They pass for straight. Leslie is a thirty-seven-year-old White lesbian with brown eyes and medium-length straight brown hair that she tucks behind her ears. Her Black partner, Sylvia, is tall and lean with stylish tortoise-shell eyeglasses and long locks that are tinged reddish-brown. When Leslie first met Sylvia, she wore her hair much shorter, and believes this aesthetic difference

---

7. Research indicates that at least among school-age children, the reverse is true. Boys' social networks are less likely than girls' to be homophilious, perhaps because boys are more likely to play in larger, less intimate groups (Maccoby 1998).

influences assumptions people make about her sexuality, and by extension, her relationship:

> I think if I was more butch, say, people might be more likely to perceive us as a couple and that could be both good and bad … It could mean I wouldn't feel as invisible at times but it could also mean that we would get more shit, you know? 'Cause people don't necessarily read either one of us alone as lesbian um, which some days is irritating to me and other days is fine.

Unless they were holding hands or kissing, when both lesbian partners expressed a stereotypically feminine style—in how they dress, wear their hair, use makeup (or not), or physically carry themselves—they felt invisible as romantic partners.

Yet, even when one partner had a traditionally "masculine" presentation of self or identified as "butch," lesbian partners sometimes still reported strangers' inability to categorize their relationship. Bryce Cook is a twenty-two-year-old White woman who identifies as queer. Bryce stands at 5'6 inches, with short dirty-blond hair and pale white skin. While she is sometimes read in public as a woman, because of her boyish looks she is more frequently read as a young man, and she is comfortable with this. Bryce's partner, Jessica Merriam, is a tall, light-skinned Black woman who also wears her hair short, and adamantly refers to herself as femme, reflecting her identification with traditionally feminine expressions of gender. Interactions with strangers in public suggest that their relationship is enigmatic to others. Bryce tells me that people have assumed that Jessica is her babysitter or have asked if Bryce is Jessica's son or little brother. These various imaginings of their relationship affirms to Bryce that many people are unable to recognize queer interracial intimacy.

> Each time its like just, "You're going out of your way to not see us as a couple." … Like maybe that pattern is easier for certain people to see than as a lesbian relationship … I'm still kind of figuring out how other people perceive us.

Bryce explains that she and Jessica hold hands in public and are affectionate in their body language or in how close they stand. In these situations, the intimacy between them is not invisible, but rather indecipherable. Strangers may recognize a connection, but attach a host of meanings to it before they consider Bryce and Jessica a romantic couple.

A Broader Lack of Recognition

Importantly, queer interracial intimacy is not only unrecognizable to strangers in public places, but it has been quite invisible to sociologists who study Black/White interracial couples. Scholars in this area have ignored the perspectives and lived experiences of gays and lesbians. Because heterosexuality has been the implicit focus, interracial intimacy in public spaces has been thought to be characterized by hypervisibility. The profound *in*visibility that lesbians and gay men sometimes experience, and the way gender shapes this invisibility, have been completely missed by these scholars. What is significant here is not only that public interraciality has been incompletely characterized, or that the full variability of interracial experiences has gone unnoticed, but that by excluding gay and lesbian interracial narratives, the social forces that shape the public lives of interracial couples have been oversimplified. When scholars study interraciality without analyzing sexuality, they assume that the "color line" is a boundary shaped mainly by White supremacy, and neglect the ways in which heteronormativity and sexism mediate the interpretation and regulation of interracial intimacy.

In this section, I have shown that in public spaces, heterosexuality creates particular problems for interracial partners. Heterosexual partners are more likely to be visibly linked as interracial couples and because they evoke historic anxieties, they are vulnerable to a type of harassment not leveled at queer interracial couples. Indeed, I argue that interraciality needs a female and a male body to become publicly legible, to be recognized as "interracial." In public, spaces that are not formally or informally coded as queer, lesbian and gay interraciality is enigmatic. It is an empty category, a sexual status without meaning. In this way, interraciality holds particular perils for heterosexual couples. Yet, at the same time, straight Black/White couples are privileged by their heterosexuality and its attendant claims to legitimacy, normalcy, and naturalness. While being heterosexual makes these couples vulnerable to harassment and violence, it also benefits them in a myriad of everyday ways.

Elsewhere I analyze in greater detail how symbolic claims to legitimacy enable heterosexual couples to create a public interracial identity that mediates stigma,[8] but in this next section I maintain my focus on the issue of social recognition by focusing on how heterosexuality mends even as it stresses public interactions. To do this, I will focus on the symbolic work that children perform in signifying heterosexuality and normative notions of family.

Analyzing Heterosexuality: Privileges and Problems

Heterosexual interracial couples occupy a complex and in many ways contradictory cultural space. Heterosexuality is not a static or meaningless element of interracial life. Each race-gender combination — whether it be a Black woman and a White man or a Black man and White woman — evokes a particular history of sexual and racial violence, each troubling to White and Black communities, albeit for different reasons. Yet this very same sexual status that renders couples conspicuous, illicit, or deviant, simultaneously offers numerous symbolic resources from which these couples derive stability and legitimacy. Children represent a core set of symbolic resources through which heterosexuals may attain normative status.

For heterosexual couples, children can perform the symbolic work of conveying "family," ensuring social recognition.[9] Hank Re-

---

8. See Steinbugler, *Everyday Interraciality*, manuscript in progress.

9. Other researchers in this area have noted that mixed-race or bir-acial children may elicit confusion or misrecognition by others in stores, restaurants or city streets when they are in the presence of only one parent (Childs 2005; Dalmage 2000; themure out what I want to say.]it nes d well stand the complexities of lesbian restaurants or city streets (Childs

nault is a forty-five-year-old White Philadelphia resident who lives with his Black wife, Mabel Renault, and their three children. Hank is a committed community activist and politician. The year before I meet him and Mabel, he ran for an elected position in city government. As we talk at his kitchen table, hanging on the wall amidst years of candid snapshots and staged family photos are mementos from his political life. As we talk he draws attention to one in particular. It is a postcard-size advertisement from an earlier campaign. The photo shows Hank in a black suit and maroon tie at the right-side of the frame looking into the camera with an intense gaze and the hint of a smile. Left of him in the photo is Mabel, who is holding their youngest child, Erwin, and between them are their two other children, Dina and Chris, who are four and six respectively. Hank's name appears across the top of the flier in blue and red letters. He tells me that he has been accused of using his brown-skinned wife and children to try to appeal to the voters of his area, many of whom are African American.[10] He has a different explanation:

> I think it's important for people to see what I'm about, who I spend my life with and who cares for me and who keeps me strong and healthy and that's that. I get slack for it. People say, "He's just showing his picture because he's married to a Black woman and these are Black folks." This says who I am. Some people can say who they are but if I meet the family, I know who they are.

Hank does not report anyone chiding him for using his heterosexuality to collect votes, but this is also a crucial subtext of the image. While it is possible that this photograph of an interracial couple

---

2005; Donst Twine and Steinbugler 2006). My analysis here focuses on the ideological work that children perform in the presence of both parents—whether and how children tie intimate partners together in the eyes of others.

10. That Hank's Black partner and children become an asset to him in his African American district reflect the ways in which racial meanings are localized. This same interracial image might be received quite differently in other parts of the city or in other geographic regions.

may alienate city residents who might otherwise vote for Hank, the image of Hank's heterosexual nuclear family performs a particular type of ideological work. It signifies respectability and legitimacy, signaling to city residents that Hank is settled, a family man who cares about his family and by extension, his community. This image of a heterosexual family, even an interracial one, reflects a form of symbolic capital to which queer partners do not have access. Children link heterosexual interracial partners together.

Wendy Julien, a heterosexual Black mother, also describes how children visually draw a couple together in public spaces. A tall woman with deep-brown skin and short locks, Wendy stands a few inches taller than her White husband Brent Isley, who has dark curly brown hair and hazel eyes. Their daughter Orianna has light brown skin and curly light brown hair. Wendy is less confident than Brent that others perceive them as a couple in social spaces. There are situations in which, "[people] don't associate one person with the other right away. Even though sometimes we're standing right next to each other. Whoever it is we're meeting, they don't expect the other person to be attached to whoever it is they're talking to." But both she and Brent explain that when they are out with Orianna, their connection feels obvious. Wendy explains that people react differently to them when they're with their child.

> Part of it is the baby factor. She's a cute baby and people are drawn and more friendly because they want to say 'hi' to the baby and they want to say 'hi' to us. So I feel like having the baby makes it like a whole little complete thing. And then it's not so much about these two people, it's about this little unit walking down the street together.

Her observations affirm that the presence of their daughter makes their heterosexual intimacy more legible to others, and evokes positive responses from those they encounter on city streets or in their neighborhood. Brent's assessment reflects a broader confidence that their relationship is generally recognizable to others. "The truth is, [in] Philadelphia, which is where we are, there's a lot of interracial couples. So I think by and large people put us together. If the two of us alone are together with our kid, most people put us together."

Gay and Lesbian Interracial Families: Hiding in Plain Sight?

If the presence of children connects heterosexual interracial partners in public spaces, does it accomplish that same work for lesbian and gay partners? In other words, do children enable gay and lesbian interracial partners to become socially recognizable as intimates and as families? In an ethnographic study of thirty-four lesbian co-parent families, Sullivan (2004) suggests that because the concept of two-mother families has yet to be easily grasped in many communities, lesbian co-parents must work harder to convey a family identity than their heterosexual counterparts. Because Sullivan's sample includes mostly White women, it is unclear how interraciality affects social recognition among gay and lesbian families. While this question requires further research, this study offers some preliminary insights. This sample includes two queer interracial families—a gay couple who had adopted two African American sons, and a lesbian couple was pregnant during the ethnographic observations. Daniel Embry, a Black gay father, described the experience he's had in public with his White partner, Shawn Tarwick, and their two African American sons. When I ask him whether he thinks that strangers see them as a family, Daniel hesitates:

> I don't know. I mean we don't hold hands. We don't do that, although we'll kiss hello or good-bye or whatever ... Actually, you know, I guess not, no. Because I guess what I started to notice particularly with the boys is that people would make any kind of configuration other than—like even when you say, "We're the parents," they still want to make it, "You're the godparents." Or you know, "The mother is still ..." or "You're the one who's watching it...." They still, they don't always get it and even if you're really straightforward about it ... We

> were at the [YMCA], the pool and ... at some point, Shawn's in the pool and I'm not. I said, "You see that man over there? That's my partner, we are the parents, the two parents." And he kept [saying], "Yes, but what's your wife's name?"

This refusal or inability to acknowledge the intimate connection between Shawn, Daniel, and their children demonstrates a lack of social recognition. The "baby factor" that Wendy and Brent experience in public spaces may not translate across sexualities. Even with children, Daniel and Shawn's intimacy is not legible to others. For gays and lesbians in public spaces, children may not be the tie that binds.

Lesbians may experience a similar lack of recognition for their unions. Sylvia Chabot is a twenty-nine-year-old Black lesbian who became pregnant through alternative insemination after our first interview and was pregnant during my six weeks of ethnographic observation. Her partner, Leslie Cobbs, is a thirty-seven-year-old White woman. According to Sylvia, they chose to use the sperm of an unknown donor, a White man, because "if we were a hetero-couple we'd have a biracial baby anyway." Anticipating their daughter's birth, Sylvia felt pessimistic about whether they would be viewed as a family.

> Soon we'll have this lovely baby with us ... People don't put us together already as a couple, and so they really won't put us together as a family. I don't know how to change that.

For Leslie, queer interraciality may be too marginal to be made comprehensible by the presence of children. She also tells me that how their family will be read by others will further depend upon their location and by the skin tone and features of their child.

Conclusion

In this essay I have explored the invisibility of queer interracial intimacy in order to examine the limitations of an analysis that theorizes interraciality by taking heterosexual subjects as it exclusive focus. My goal has been to view interraciality through a broader lens that considers both a wider set of interracial experiences—both heterosexual and queer—and a more expansive understanding of the social forces that structure visible sexualities. Exploring interracial narratives, I have demonstrated that the public experiences of heterosexual interracial couples are often marked by social recognition, and for Black men and White women, hypervisibility. I have contrasted this with the more pronounced invisibility that queer Black/White couples experience, (especially lesbians), and have explored how gender mediates public experiences of interraciality. Juxtaposing these narratives, I argue that heterosexuality creates particular problems and particular privileges for interracial couples, and illustrate this through a discussion of children as a symbolic resource. This work affirms the need for further explorations of queer interracial lives, including those outside of the Black/White paradigm.

In making this critique, I am not suggesting that we abandon analysis of heterosexual interraciality but that we begin to think about it differently. This starts by conceptualizing interraciality as a sexual status. If we accept heterosexual Black/White interracial partners as inhabiting a particular sexual status, we are able to see that their experiences in public spaces (and also with families, coworkers, friends, etc.) are not influenced solely by the "color line" and their transgression across it, but also by structures of heteronormativity and sexism which simultaneously aggravate and ameliorate racial differences. Heteronormativity, sexism, and White supremacy are interconnected and interdependent. While we can understand the public harassment that heterosexual interracial couples have historically received as the penalty for crossing the color line in racist society, we should also consider this harassment as the consequence of violating heterosexual norms of monoraciality. For disrupting heterosexual norms, straight Black/White couples have, at times, been denied many fundamental privileges of heterosexuality—the right to characterize their intimacy as "natural," to show affection without threat of harassment, to marry, etc. In other words, the problem of interraciality is not only about the color line. It is also about a social system that rewards and disadvantages intimate bodies according to their gender and sexuality.

Conceptualizing interraciality as a sexual status creates space for the analysis of lesbian and gay interraciality. In this essay, I've explored how public assumptions of heteronormativity and monoraciality render queer interracial couples unrecognizable, and showed that queer partners may avoid harassment by strategically cloaking themselves in invisibility and passing as heterosexual friends. Their narratives spur further questions. How does sexual identity affect other realms of interracial intimacy? Do lesbian, gay, and heterosexual partners have similar strategies for negotiating racial difference within their relationship? Does sexual identity affect the ways in which interracial partners conceptualize racial difference? Does it affect how they construct identities vis-à-vis interraciality? These questions must be a core priority of future research on interracial intimacy.

Bibliography

Baca Zinn, M., and B. Thornton Dill. 1996. Theorizing difference from multiracial feminism. *Feminist Studies* 22 2:321–33.

Brickell, C. 2000. Heroes and invaders: gay and lesbian pride parades and the public/private distinction in New Zealand media accounts. *Gender, Place & Culture: A Journal of Feminist Geography* 7:163–179.

Childs, E.C. 2005. *Navigating interracial borders: black-white couples and their social worlds.* New Brunswick, NJ: Rutgers University Press.

Cohen, C. J. 1997. Punks, bulldaggers and welfare queens: the radical potential of queer politics. *GLQ* 3:437–465.

Collins, P.H. 1991. *Black feminist thought: knowledge, consciousness, and the politics of empowerment.* New York: Routledge.

Crenshaw, K. 1991. Mapping the margins: intersectionality, identity politics, and violence against women. *Stanford Law Review* 43 (6):1241–99.

Dalmage, H. M. 2000. *Tripping on the color line: black-white multiracial families in a racially divided world.* New Brunswick, NJ.: Rutgers University Press.

D'Emilio, J. and E. B. Freedman. 1988. *Intimate matters: a history of sexuality in America.* New York: Harper and Row.

Dow, B. J. 2001. Ellen, television, and the politics of gay and lesbian visibility. *Critical Studies in Media Communication* 18:123–141.

Drake, S.C. and H. R. Cayton. 1945. *Black metropolis: a study of Negro life in a northern city* Vol. 1. New York: Harper & Row.

Evans, D.T. 1993. *Sexual citizenship: the material construction of sexualities.* New York: Routledge.

Fogg-Davis, H. G. 2006. Theorizing black lesbians within black feminism: a critique of same-race street harassment. *Politics & Gender* 2:57–76.

Frankenberg, R. 1993. *White women, race matters: the social construction of whiteness.* Minneapolis: University of Minnesota Press.

Gross, L. P. 2001. *Up from invisibility: lesbians, gay men, and the media in America.* New York: Columbia University Press.

Higginbotham, A.L. 1978. *In the matter of color: race and the American legal process.* New York: Oxford University Press.

Hodes, M.E. 1997. *White women, black men: illicit sex in the nineteenth-century South.* New Haven, CT: Yale University Press.

Hernandez, D. Young and out: anything but safe. *Colorlines Magazine.* December 2004.

Johnson, C. 2002. Heteronormative citizenship and the politics of passing. *Sexualities* 5:317–336.

Lasser, J. and D. Tharinger. 2003. Visibility management in school and beyond: a qualitative study of gay, lesbian, bisexual youth. *Journal of Adolescence* 26:233–244.

Maccoby, E. 1998. *The Two Sexes: Growing Up Apart, Coming Together.* Cambridge, MA: Harvard University Press.

McNamara, R.P., M. Tempnis, and B. Walton. 1999. *Crossing the line: interracial couples in the South.* Westport, CT: Greenwood Press.

Porterfield, E. 1978. *Black and white mixed marriages*. Chicago: Nelson-Hall.

Rosenblatt, P.C., T.A. Karis, and R. Powell. 1995. *Multiracial couples: black and white voices*. Thousand Oaks, CA: Sage Publications.

Romano, R.C. 2003. *Race mixing: black-white marriage in postwar America*. Cambridge, MA: Harvard University Press.

Root, M.R.R. 2001. *Love's revolution: interracial marriage*. Philadelphia, PA.: Temple University Press.

Rothman, B.K. 2005. *Weaving a family: untangling race and adoption*. Boston: Beacon Press.

Smith, B. 1998. *The truth that never hurts: writings on race, gender, and freedom*. New Brunswick, NJ: Rutgers University Press.

Steinbugler, A. C. 2005. Visibility as privilege and danger: heterosexual and same-sex interracial intimacy in the 21st century. *Sexualities* 8: 425–443.

_____. 2007. *'Race has always been more than just race': gender, sexuality, and the negotiation of race in interracial relationships*. Ph.D. diss., Temple University.

Sullivan, Maureen. 2004. *The Family of Woman: Lesbian Mothers, Their Children, and the Undoing of Gender*. Berkeley: University of California Press.

United States Census. 2000. Hispanic Origin and Race of Coupled Households: 2000.

Twine, F.W. and A.C. Steinbugler. 2006. The gap between "whites" and "whiteness": interracial intimacy and racial literacy. *Du Bois Review* 3.

Walters, S. D. 2001. *All the rage: the story of gay visibility in America*. Chicago: University of Chicago Press.

Warner, M. 1993. *Fear of a queer planet: queer politics and social theory*. Minneapolis: University of Minnesota Press.

Wright, K. Risking it all to find safety. *Colorlines Magazine*. May/June 2008.

Chapter 7

Unequally Yoked:
How Willing Are Christians to
Engage in Interracial and
Interfaith Dating?

George Yancey with Emily J. Hubbard & Amy Smith

Introduction

There are reasons to believe that interfaith romances are more accepted than interracial ones (Gordon, 1964; Spickard, 1989). In a post-modern society, differing religions may not be considered an obstacle when one is seeking a romantic partner. However, we still live in a highly racialized society (Bonilla-Silva, 2001; Emerson & Smith, 2000; Van Ausdale & Feagin, 2001) and, as such, racial differences still matter. Thus, while individuals may prefer to date and/or marry someone of their own faith, they may be even more insistent on finding a person of a similar race. Indeed, in another chapter, one of the authors demonstrates that individuals dating over the internet are more open to dating individuals outside of their faith than outside of their race (Yancey, Unpublished paper).

For a variety of reasons, Christians with a high degree of religiosity should be especially hesitant to become romantically involved with individuals who are not of their same faith. For example, dating someone outside of one's faith may challenge one's own belief system. Furthermore, interfaith marriages produce challenges in raising children in the Christian tradition. When individuals are not able to easily find a partner within a desired endogamous group then they may become more open to exogamy (Davidson & Wilman, 2002; Spickard, 1989). In the United States, finding a member within the endogamous group is not a problem for Christians as Christianity is clearly the dominant religion. Approximately 78.9 percent of all individuals in the United States identify themselves as Christians.[1] Therefore, for Christians it is not difficult to find others who share a Christian faith. Although there are distinctive Christian groups that may also serve as potential religious barriers, even subgroups of Christians are unlikely to be so small as to discourage individuals within those traditions from easily finding individuals of similar faiths.[2]

Among the highly religious, it is quite possible that aversion to interfaith romances is greater than towards Christian interracial unions. They may incorporate the values of Christianity so deeply that they are uncomfortable with the idea of dating outside of their faith. It is logical to conclude that because individuals of different races can also share similar religious values, highly religious Christians may be open to seeking out a romantic alliance with Christians of other races, as long as they share their faith. In this work we will problematize this assertion. The three authors of this chapter are Christians who consider ourselves to have high religiosity. Thus, we

---

1. This is according to the 2006 General Social Survey.

2. For example, Christianity can be broadly defined into Catholic, mainline Protestant, and conservative Protestant. It can be fairly argued that although there are distinctions within these three groups, those distinctions are not powerful enough to create religious dissonance. Thus, a Baptist may date an Assembly of God member or a Presbyterian may date a Lutheran without much religious conflict. Of these three groups, the smallest is the Mainline Protestants who make up 26.4 percent of the United States (University, 2005). Even this number is deceiving, as members of such groups tend to be located in northeast and north central parts of the United States. High concentration makes it more likely that mainline Protestants can find other Mainline Protestants for romance. Lack of proximity probably is not a reason for Christians to engage in interfaith relationship for all but few Christians in the United States.

produce a certain level of an "insider" view into this issue. However, we will augment our more personal perceptions with results based on quantitative data gathered at an internet dating website.

Instructions on Interfaith Dating

There is a plethora of Christian sources that condemn interfaith romance (Clark, 2000; Cloud & Townsend, 2000; Dobson, 1995; Frazier, 2002; Ham, Wieland, & Batten, 2000; Myra, 1994; Phillips & Phillips, 2006; Rice & Rice, 1981). Such romances are seen as troublesome since they may discourage a Christian from adhering to his/her faith (Clark, 2000; Cloud & Townsend, 2000). Indeed, each of us experienced Christian influences that discouraged us from entering into interfaith relationships.

> As for marrying a non-Christian, that was never ever an option in my life. I couldn't ever have had a relationship with a boy who wasn't a Christian.... I'm sure my mother probably had something to do with it—she probably emphasized that part in the Bible where it said "do not be unequally yoked." I'm sure I heard it in sermons and I know I heard it in youth group and in a couple of "single girl" bible studies. Even though I can fuzzily recall hearing it taught, I don't remember the first time I learned it—I feel like it's something I've always "known." (Hubbard)
>
> When I described anyone of the opposite gender (whether I was interested in dating him or not), the first question my parents, my friends, my church leaders, and even some of my professors asked was if he was a Christian or not. The second question was always about how committed he was to his Christian faith. After that came the typical questions about appearance, family background, personality, manners, etc. Not only was I encouraged to date within my faith, I was discouraged to date outside of it. Those who influenced me the most

told me to set my priorities, and at the top of my priority list, I had to make sure that I was focusing on my relationship with Christ ... Everyone who cared about me said the same thing: Christianity overshadows all the other details in a dating relationship. After that, I could have as much diversity as I desired in a date or future spouse. (Smith)

Having not married until my early 30's, I attended several single and college ministries where the topic of dating outside of my faith came up. Each and every time I was discouraged from doing so. Typically, I would be reminded that to date someone outside of my faith was to tamper with my own faith. The non-Christian would be likely to influence me away from my faith. Furthermore, I was discouraged from engaging in "missionary dating" or dating someone who is not a Christian as a way to bring them into the faith. There were a few times in which I saw this happen but I was taught that what would be more likely to happen was that the Christian would fall away from his/her faith. (Yancey)

These experiences are not unique to us. As we have talked with other Christians, we have found that they, too, have been warned against dating non-Christians. These experiences coupled with the above mentioned literature indicate that prohibition of dating non-Christians is a nearly universal instruction given to those who are in a conservative Protestant faith.[3] In fact, our search of primary Christian literature failed to turn up even a single case in which the author positively supported the idea of dating a non-Christian. Christians clearly have received a uniform message opposing interfaith romance from their relevant authority leaders.

---

3. While the prohibition may not be as strong in other versions of Christianity or non-Christian religions, there is evidence that it is powerfully present outside of conservative Protestantism (Frame, 2004; Silverstein, 2001).

Instructions on Interracial Dating

Historically, there has been a great deal of Christian resistance against interracial romance (Buswell, 1964; Romano, 2003). Furthermore, there may be elements within Christianity that promote notions of racial purity (Jordan, 1968; Van Der Post, 1955; Wilmore, 1972). Yet, none of us can explicitly remember official Christian teaching against interracial dating. In fact, we have often enjoyed multiracial Christian interaction. For each of us, our Christian lifestyle has been compatible with mixing with those of different races and cultures.

> And I kept going on mission trips to inner cities that reinforced the ideas of black people not as poor people but as equals and individuals ... I was— ... really interested in knowing black people—due in part to those mission trips but also to my African American literature class. And I moved in with an older black lady, and started going to an early service at a Missionary Baptist church (a predominately black church). (Hubbard)
> In the middle of mostly white, Southern suburb, the Christian school I attended included a large population of international boarding students. My family loved hosting some of these students during the holidays and summer months. We kept over 25 students from four continents and nearly ten countries throughout my middle and high school years. With each new person that stayed in our home, we made an effort to learn something about their culture and teach them something about ours. (Smith)
> When I served as a campus minister, one of my duties was the development of a Christian voice to the African-Americans on campus. However, I was not relegated to serving only African-Americans as I also was responsibility for the white students as well. While there was not always a great deal of overlap, the ministry became

> a source of spiritual support for members of both races. This was for me an especially rich time of multiracial contact as I operated between both racial cultures on a consistent basis. (Yancey)

Although we benefited from our multiracial experiences, we still experienced informal resistance within our Christian circles against interracial dating. This resistance was especially clear to the two authors who have gone on to interracially marry.

> After we were married, we had some of my older sister's friends over, and one friend's husband believes that intermarriage is wrong. She said he wasn't a racist, just a bad exegeticist ... Of course, we were already married by then, so it wasn't like he could do anything about it. Even in his book, I'm sure divorce is worse than intermarriage. (Hubbard)
>
> I remember being a part of a singles ministry, and every time a Black woman started attending the meeting the singles pastors would comment on what a good match we (her and this new member) would be. They never did so when a non-Black woman joined the ministry. When I did start dating a White woman, I heard that some of the singles in the ministry thought that it was wrong and hoped that we would break up. It was very disheartening. (Yancey)

Our search of the literature has revealed very few primary, contemporary Christian sources that condemn interracial dating and several that support it (Frazier, 2002; Keener, 2002; Myra, 1994). However, these experiences indicate that formal Christian support for interracial relationships may be negated by informal sanctions against them. It is plausible that Christians do not overtly oppose interracial relationships due to a fear of being labeled racist and yet they do not act on their stated intentions.[4]

---

4. It should also be recognized that the relatively low number of interracial marriages among highly committed Christians can make this an

Christianity and Racism

While there is still conflict concerning the issues surrounding interracial marriage, condemnation of these types of marriages is no longer popular. Such condemnation is commonly seen as an example of prejudice. Although most Christians will not admit to being racist, Allport (1966) argues that churchgoers in our country have higher levels of racial, ethnic, and religious prejudice than non-churchgoers. Roberts (2004), however, contends that this is not always the case. He defines two types of church members—those who are intrinsically religious and those who are extrinsically religious. Intrinsically religious people are more likely to join a church because faith is a meaningful and integral part of their lives (Roberts, 2003: 254). As part of their intrinsic religiosity, this person has compassion, and love for other people (Jackson & Hunsberger, 1999). Extrinsically religious individuals focus more their utilitarian gains from belonging to a church group (Allport, 1966). In other words, they choose to be religious because of the label, not because of actual belief. When the data was broken down into intrinsic and extrinsic groups by factors such as church attendance, the extrinsic group was highly prejudiced while the intrinsic group was one of the least prejudiced groups in the entire study (Batson, Schoenrade, & Ventis, 1993; Kirkpatrick, 1993). Those who were seriously committed to Christianity by living a distinct lifestyle and attending church on a regular basis were far less prejudiced than those who claimed Christianity, but rarely attended church and/or did not allow their religious faith to change how they lived their lives.

It is possible that the decision of Christians to be willing to interracially date is linked to their adherence to church attendance.

---

unimportant issue to most Christian leaders. This tendency is exacerbated by the fact that most Christian churches are racially homogenous (Chaves, 1999; Emerson & Smith, 2000). Thus, Christian leaders do not address issues of racial exclusion in romantic relationships, which provides a subtle signal that such exclusion is acceptable.

Contemporary Christian literature prohibits interfaith, but not interracial, dating. Furthermore, our experiences show that there is an abundance of verbal Christian instruction against interfaith dating, but little overt instruction against interracial dating. Thus, one would expect that Christians who are regular church attendees would also prioritize the faith, and not the race, of their dating partners.

Why Christians May Not Interracially Date

However, even committed Christians may be hesitant to interracially date. Theories of symbolic racism (Sears, 1988; Sniderman & Tetlock, 1986) indicate that Americans can practice racism through symbolic categories. By placing very high emphasis on "moral codes" and especially traditional American values like individualism, success, respect for authority, and conservative morality, White symbolic racists are able to manipulate these values to allow them to express disapproval towards people of color through a belief that people of color frequently do not perform according to the moral codes or traditional ideals. This ideology is not far from overt racism, as Daniels's (1997) look at White supremacist discourse finds that its message is relatively close to mainstream perceptions. In this discourse, she finds that Black males are portrayed as criminal, incompetent, and sexually out of control while Black female stereotypes highlight the morally suspect welfare mother and irresponsible sexuality. Yet by focusing on seemingly non-racist discourse, members of the majority group can avoid admitting to racism while justifying non-attraction to non-Whites.

This non-attraction may be more relevant to White Christians. There is evidence that adherence to notions of racial purity can be found within Christian ideology. Wilmore (1972) argues that the strong emphasis in some elements of Protestant theology on moral purity is often symbolically linked to notions of perfection. Racial purity can symbolically be seen as a path to perfection. Jordan (1968) also points out that within Christian theology "white" and purity are linked. This is reinforced by Van Der Post's (1955) argument that attempts at inner purity can create the tendency of Whites to perceive "black" as evil and lead to an aversion to African-Americans. Therefore, White Christians may have a powerful ideological incentive to latch onto symbolic notions of racial purity, if they can find non-racist justifications (such as not being attracted to non-Whites) for their actions.

Thus, it is unclear whether such symbolic aspects of racial purity are more powerful than the potential positive effects of Christianity in limiting prejudice. However, even without a symbolic racism effect, Christians in the U.S. in general may be more willing to engage in interfaith, rather than interracial, dating since individuals in the U.S. generally favor interfaith over interracial romance (Gordon, 1964; Spickard, 1989). This tendency alone may make it more difficult for Christians to seek out interracial, rather than interfaith, romances. Such a tendency would affect both White and non-White Christians, while the forces of symbolic racism discussed above is likely to only affect White Christians.

More than any other issues relating to race, interracial marriage and dating may bring out hidden or forgotten prejudices (Lewis & Yancey, 1995; Myra, 1994; Stember, 1976). Measures of overt racism are not the best way to capture expressions of Christian symbolic racism. If Christians can find "biblical" reasons to resist interracial unions, then assessments of their attitudes and actions towards interracial dating may be a better barometer of the degree of racial prejudice in the Christian community. Christians who internalize the morals they gain from religious belief may be likely to accept people of other races because of Christian teachings on personhood and equality. However, it is also possible that the ideas of racial purity within the Christian community, especially the White Christian community, may persuade even serious Christians to resist interracial dating. Based on our personal experiences, we designed an empirical study to elucidate the ways these factors might interact to shape the likelihood of interracial dating among Christians.

Procedures

We use an assessment of personal advertisements to measure the willingness of Christians to engage in interracial and interfaith dating. Previous studies have used newspaper personal advertisements to measure adherence to traditional gender roles (Campos, Otta, & Siqueira, 2002; Smith, Waldorf, & Trembath, 1990; Toro-Morn & Sprecher, 2003), understand the nature of courtship (Montini & Ovrebro, 1990), and determine which qualities make individuals more attractive to prospective romantic partners (Pawlowski & Koziel, 2002). Yancey and Yancey (1997, 1998) also utilized personal advertisements in several newspapers and magazines to explore the propensity of interracial daters to offer or desire relational assets. Their research is limited as they examined only newspapers in a few areas of the United States and specialty periodicals to oversample for individuals seeking interracial relationships. This work compared interracial daters to other daters, but cannot provide insight into who interracially dates.

Lynn and Bolig (1985) have pointed out three advantages of using personal advertisements to research romantic relationships: 1) subjects are not aware of being studied, 2) subjects are studied in a naturalistic rather than a laboratory setting, and 3) subjects in the sample tend to be representative of the general population. The second advantage is acutely important in studying social exogamy because the naturalness of the setting helps control for social desirability effects. Individuals who desire to present themselves as socially tolerant may not indicate to an interviewer/survey an unwillingness to outdate. However, there are real consequences to such an evasion when one places a personal advertisement.

Recent studies have utilized internet personal advertisements to explore romantic relationships (Kaufman & Phua, 2003; Luehrmann, 2004; Phua, 2002; Phua & Kaufman, 2003). Internet advertisements are superior to newspaper or magazine personal advertisements for capturing dating preferences. An advantage of internet personal advertisements is that advertisers are directly asked to indicate which racial/religious groups they will date. Since there is little room in a newspaper advertisement, an advertiser may omit his/her racial/religious preferences and merely filter out unwanted races. Furthermore, by sampling relatively few advertisements from many different areas of the country, as opposed to sampling a high number of advertisements from a few selected newspapers, more generalized assertions become possible. Finally, using personal advertisements neutralizes the concern of measuring the opportunity of individuals to interracially date. Since a person directly indicates his/her willingness to outdate, advertisers with non-diverse social networks can reveal a willingness to outdate even if they do not have the opportunity to do so.

Data and Methods

Data from this project was gathered from the Yahoo! Personals website. While there are other personal advertisements websites (i.e. Match.com, Lavalife), they tend to cater to specific dating pool niches. Yahoo! is a popular search engine attracting a wide range of individuals. While the Yahoo! website allows individuals to search for potential romantic matches in the United States and Canada, this current research endeavor is limited to only those in the United States. We set the search engine so that there were no restrictions upon the potential daters selected and included those without a photo. Thus, any dater in the United States with internet access is a potential respondent.[5]

---

5. It should also be acknowledged that the potential respondent has to be willing to look for dating partners online. It is possible that this is not a random subset of all daters. There is nothing we can do to account for the possibility that online daters systematically differ from non-online daters in our society. However, Sautter et. al. (2006) finds that while individuals who date online do differ in sex, race, age education, income and religiosity from the general population, these demographic differences largely disappear once internet use and marital status is controlled. This research provides more confidence in the generalizability of research using online daters to the rest of the dating population.

The Yahoo! website allows potential daters to search as far as 250 miles from any given city, but does not allow for a random sample of the entire United States. Since a random probability sample is not possible, we utilized a stratified sampling technique. We used GSS categories to create nine regions (Pacific, Mountain, West South Central, West North Central, East South Central, East North Central, New England, South Atlantic, and Middle Atlantic). The largest city in each region was automatically selected. The rest of the cities were divided into those with more than 25,000 inhabitants and those with less than 25,000 inhabitants.[6] Three cities were randomly chosen in each region from the first group of cities and five cities from the second group. Thus, nine cities were chosen from each region, allowing for regional and city size diversity.

From the largest city in the region, forty dater profiles were chosen (twenty men and twenty women).[7] From each medium size city (more than 25,000 inhabitants, but not the largest city in the region), ten dater profiles were chosen (five men and five women). From each small city (less than 25,000 inhabitants), four profiles were chosen (two men and two women). If a particular city did not have any dater profiles on Yahoo! then an appropriately sized city in the region was randomly chosen to take its place. After the advertisements were coded, we did not have enough advertisements of Blacks, Hispanics and Asians to make useful cross-racial comparisons. So an oversample of these groups was collected[8] by randomly select-

---

6. The 25,000 inhabitant cutoff was used for convenience. Census data provided the listing of cities over 25,000 and allowed me to conduct the sampling. While the 25,000 cutoff is somewhat arbitrary, it does allow me to have some control over city size in the larger sample.

7. All of the advertisements are of individuals seeking heterosexual relationships. It makes little sense to confound possible findings by incorporating sexual preference differences. It is possible that some of the advertisements captured those who are bisexual, but we have no way of determining the extent to which this may be true.

8. The oversample was done in January of 2006, only six months after the original sampling. The questionnaire used was exactly the same as before. There is no reason to think that the general dating patterns of the daters of Yahoo! were any different six months later than they had been be-

ing two members of each racial group (a male and female) from each large city. Second, we randomly choose one of the medium and small size cities in each region and selected two members of each racial group from those cities. If members of that group were not found, we randomly choose another medium or small city. It was not always the case that we could find all six daters in the group of medium or small cities. This added a total of forty-eight black, forty-six Hispanic and forty-one Asian daters to the sample. In all, 1,060 individuals comprised the sample. Since this is not a random sample we compensated for the non-randomness by weighing the data by the information in the U.S. Census for each region and by city size.[9]

Variables

Each dater indicated his/her own race and races he/she is willing to date. The racial categories are African-American (Black), Asian, Caucasian (White), East Indian, Hispanics/Latino, Middle Eastern, Native American, Pacific Islander, Interracial and Other. The dater could pick as many, or as few, racial groups that he/she wanted to date or could pick the category "any." Daters picking all available racial groups as prospective dating partners also fit the "any" group. Daters could also indicate that they wanted to date racially endogenously by indicating only their race in this profile section. Daters refusing to indicate their own race or the races of the individuals they wanted to date are excluded since it would be impossible to determine their willingness to interracially date.

Each dater also indicated his/her own religious affiliation and the religious affiliation of those he/she is willing to date. We included those who picked Christian, Christian/Protestant, Christ-

---

fore. Thus, I have confidence that the oversample only adds to the knowledge this data can provide about racial minorities seeking to find an opposite-sex romantic partner.

9. Details of how the data was weighed can be seen in Yancey (2007).

ian/Catholic, and Christian/other in this study. These Christians had the option of picking "any" in this category for a desired partner, of picking one or all of the four above categories (and are only willing to date other Christians) or of including some of the non-Christian categories in their preference. This allows us to determine which Christians are willing to date outside of their faith (although they still may choose to not date members of certain religious groups), Christians willing to date those of all different religious groups, and Christians who are not willing to engage in interfaith dating. Christians who refused to indicate which religious groups they are willing to date are excluded since it would be impossible to determine their willingness to engage in interfaith dating. To compare the propensity of symbolic racism against societal tendency to favor interfaith over interracial relationships, we will test the tendency of White Christians to date outside of their race and faith as compared to the entire population of daters.

Results

In Table 1, we examined the different tendencies of Christians to date regardless of race and regardless of religious faith. Higher percentages indicate a greater tendency of Christians to date individuals of either all races or all faiths. When we look at all Christians, we found that they are almost 50 percent more likely to limit who they date by race than they are by their faith. This pattern is less pronounced, but similar when we look at Christians who attend church at least monthly and/or at least weekly. Religiosity does not eliminate the propensity of Christians to emphasize limitations of race over limitations of religious faith in persons they date. It is worth noting that the difference in the percentage of Christians who date regardless of race and those who date regardless of religion does decrease as church attendance increases. However, the difference remains significant even when examining Christians who attend church at least weekly. This same pattern is upheld when we look only at White Christians. White Christians emphasize limiting who they date by race more than who they date by faith, al-

Table 1 Comparisons of the Willingness of Christians to Date Others Regardless of Race and the Willingness of Christians to Date Others Regardless of Religion

	Will Date Regardless of Race	Will Date Regardless of Religion
All Races		
All Christians	43.2%	62.3%[d]
(N = 1,371)		
Attend Church at Least Monthly	37.1%	49.8%[d]
(N = 531)		
Attend Church at Least Weekly	33.2%	41.8%[b]
(N = 327)		
Only Whites		
All Christians	42.5%	65.9%[d]
(N = 957)		
Attend Church at Least Monthly	34.0%	50.7%[d]
(N = 310)		
Attend Church at Least Weekly	35.2%	45.3%[a]
(N = 172)		
Only Non-Whites		
All Christians	44.9%	54.0%[c]
(N = 411)		
Attend Church at Least Monthly	41.6%	48.1%
(N = 219)		
Attend Church at Least Weekly	31.2%	37.2%
(N = 154)		

a. significantly different from "will date regardless of race" at .1 level
b. significantly different from "will date regardless of race" at .05 level
c. significantly different from "will date regardless of race" at .01 level
d. significantly different from "will date regardless of race" at .001 level

though once again the difference between the two factors does decrease as church attendance increases.

However, among Christians of color this pattern is not upheld. While Christians of color in general are more willing to limit themselves racially than religiously, this pattern does not hold for Christians of color who attend church at least monthly. Here, the differences are not significant in spite of the fact that a higher percentage of Christians of color limit themselves racially than religiously in whom they will date. Among Christians of color who attend church at least monthly, there is not much difference between their willingness to date outside of their faith than from White Christians, however, Christians of color are more willing to date outside of their race than White Christians. Christians of color who attend church at least monthly are highly likely to racially screen who they will date, but are also highly likely to screen who they will date religiously. Thus, Christians of color who exhibit some degree of religiosity are more likely to adhere to the priority of emphasizing the faith of their prospective romantic partner than the race of that partner than White Christians.

However, the results in Table 1 do not tell us about the degree to which Christians may limit who they date racially or religiously. It is theoretically possible that many Christians open to dating those of other faiths are willing to date few of the non-Christians categories while Christians who limit who they date by race only eliminate a few of the other racial groups. It still may be possible that the religion of prospective partners is generally more important to Christians than the race of those partners.

In Table 2, we look at the propensity of Christians to date only their own race or only other Christians. In other words, we are looking at racial or religious endogamy at its higher level. Higher percentages indicate a greater number of Christians only willing to date those of their own race or are only willing to date other Christians. We found that 32 percent of all Christians in our weighted sample were only willing to date those of their own race compared to 28.5 percent of all Christians who are only willing to date other Christians. This difference is significant at the .05 level. However, as reported frequency of church attendance increases, this relationship is reversed and Christians with more religiosity are more likely to date only Christians than they are to date only those of their race.

Separating the Christian sample by Whites and non-Whites indicates that this tendency is driven by the propensity of non-Whites to value dating only Christians rather than only members of their own race. Among all White Christians, there is a higher tendency to date only Whites than only Christians and as we look at White

Table 2 Comparisons of the Willingness of Christians to Date Only Own Race and the Willingness of Christians to Date Only Christians

	Will Only Date Own Race	Will Only Date Christians
All Christians	32.0%	28.5%[a]
	(1,368)	(1,339)
Attend Church	30.0%	40.5%[c]
at Least Monthly	(529)	(515)
Attend Church	32.6%	44.7%[b]
at Least Weekly	(325)	(311)
Only Whites		
All Christians	36.8%	27.2%[c]
	(957)	(944)
Attend Church	36.0%	42.5%
at Least Monthly	(310)	(309)
Attend Church	38.7%	44.9%
at Least Weekly	(172)	(170)
Only Non-Whites		
All Christians	20.7%	31.9%[c]
	(411)	(392)
Attend Church	21.5%	37.8%[c]
at Least Monthly	(219)	(204)
Attend Church	25.9%	44.9%[c]
at Least Weekly	(154)	(138)

a. significantly different from "will date regardless of race" at .05 level
b. significantly different from "will date regardless of race" at .01 level
c. significantly different from "will date regardless of race" at .001 level

Christians who are more frequent church attendees, we find non-significant relationships between the two tendencies. This does not change as we limit our sample to only White Christians who attend church at least monthly and at least weekly. Generally, White Christians are as willing to be highly exclusive racially as to be highly exclusive religiously, regardless of their level of religiosity. Yet, among Christians of color, the propensity to date only Christians is higher than the propensity to date only within their own race at all three levels of religiosity. It is quite clear that Christians of color are significantly more likely to limit themselves to only Christians than to limit themselves to only people of their own race. Thus, we have evidence that Christians of color are more likely to adhere to the intrinsic Christian values of emphasizing religious exclusiveness over racial exclusiveness.

Discussion

Despite the primary sources and our experiences in Christian college and singles groups suggesting that Christians are more concerned with interfaith dating rather than interracial dating, the evidence from this study indicates that White Christians are more likely to place racial constraints, rather than religious boundaries, on who they date. It is a tendency that does not change as White Christians experience higher religiosity, although Whites with high religiosity are less likely to engage in both interfaith and interracial dating than their less religious peers. Contrary to what one might expect, increased church attendance fails to ameliorate the propensity of White Christians to only date inside of their race.

The story is different for Christians of color. Measurements of all Christians of color indicate a general higher tendency to emphasize racial expectations over religious expectations. This tendency seems to be in keeping with the values of the larger society. However, religiosity reduces this particular societal effect. It can be argued that Christians of color who become more serious about their faith are more likely to reject interfaith dating as primary Christian literature has emphasized. Furthermore, Christians of color are also more likely to date only Christians than to date only members of their own race at every level of church attendance. As we predicted, non-White Christians have less incentive to avoid interracial dating than members of the majority group.

This research indicates that Christians are generally more likely to prioritize the race over the faith of their potential romantic partner. It is important to consider not only what social groups state as their values but also what behaviors members of the group engage in.[10] This work also suggests that the religious life of White and non-White Christians differ from each other. While both White and non-White Christians show reluctance towards interfaith and interracial dating, White Christians are especially reluctant to interracially date. Somehow, racial exclusiveness has a more core position in the Christian faith of the majority group than it does for Christians of color. Since religious expressions are connected to the cultural atmosphere that shapes them, this cross-racial contrast may be reflective of the larger, racially-based cultural differences in the U.S.

For example, some research suggests that European-Americans prioritize Eurocentric cultural values over those of people of color (Dyer, 2002; Twine, 1997). People of color may be less likely to focus on such an in-group tendency since they are regularly reminded that they possess an inferior social position to majority group members. Since majority group members are more likely to possess the cultural and phenotypical attributes that conforms to such Eurocentrism, a higher in-group romantic preference among majority group members, relative to minority group members, seems quite plausible. Different adaptations of a Christian belief system may reflect or intensify this cross-racial difference as European-American Christians develop subtle theological belief systems that reinforce racial endogamy more powerfully than the theological belief systems developed among Christians of color.

---

10. The importance of understanding the difference between what individuals state is important and what is actually important to them can also be seen in research by Emerson and Sikkink (Forthcoming) indicating that educated Whites are more likely to indicate that they support integrated neighborhoods and schools and yet are more likely to live in segregated neighborhoods and send their kids to racially monolithic schools. These findings hold up even after important social and demographic controls have been applied to the results.

Conclusion

A great deal of emphasis has been placed by Christians on the evils of interfaith dating, and of becoming "unequally yoked" while almost none, in recent years, has been placed upon interracial dating. However, White Christians are more likely to use race, rather than religion, as a screening mechanism in their dating patterns. The power of sentiments against interracial romance is such that Christians adhere to those sentiments even though there is little evidence that suggests that they are overtly taught to avoid interracial dating. Because there are few overt cues given to Christians telling them to avoid interracial dating, it is likely that there are informal signals that Christians receive that discourage racial exogamy. Our experiences illustrate some of these potential signals. While these experiences illustrate only a few, relatively minor ways that informal romances may occur, there may be a cumulative effect of such occurrences that are more influential than the overt prohibitions that Christians receive about interfaith dating. Future qualitative research may use experiences like ours to more fully discover how such signals operate to maintain racially endogamous norms.

We documented evidence that Christians are more likely to be racially restrictive on who they will date than restrictive on their religious concerns. However, there is less evidence that Christians are more willing to date only those of their own race than to date those of their own religion. This distinction may be due to the fact that relatively few individuals limit themselves only to those of their own racial group, but it is still common to exclude certain racial groups. However, Christian literature typically admonishes adherents to avoid dating anyone outside of the Christian faith. As the evidence of this research suggests, this admonishment makes it highly likely that Christians who are restrictive at all about religious exogamy will only date other Christians.[11] Such an either/or

---

11. For example, 28.5 percent of all White Christians will only date Christians and 65.9 percent of them will date a partner regardless of religion. Adding these two percentages together indicates that these two groups

stance on interfaith dating is different from the approach many individuals have towards interracial dating, in that many people are willing to date some, but not all, members who are not in their racial group.

It is worth thinking about why people of color are more likely to adhere to the notion that faith is more important than race as it concerns prospective dating partners. Superficially, it is tempting to believe that because race is more salient in the life of people of color, that Christians of color would be more likely to take racial factors into consideration in who they will date. However, such an assertion ignores the relative social positions of the distinctive racial groups in our society. Even in our contemporary society, there is evidence that majority group members retain a favored place relative to other racial groups (Bonilla-Silva, 2003; Carr, 1997; Feagin, 2000; Hacker, 1995; McIntosh, 2002; Oliver & Shapiro, 1995). Maintaining notions of racial purity can enable majority group members to protect their dominant racial position. Given this reality, it is not surprising that majority group members are generally less supportive of interracial romance than people of color (Aldridge, 1978; Fang, Sidanius, & Pratto, 1998; Knox, Zusman, Buffington, & Hemphill, 2000; Lewis & Yancey, 1995). Thus, White daters may place a higher degree of emphasis in racial exclusivity than daters of color. This can free Christians of color to prioritize fidelity to their religious commitments over adherence to societal racial norms.

There is reason to believe that European-Americans occupy the highest place in our racial hierarchy (Fang et al., 1998; Spickard, 1989; Yancey, 2003). White Christians may practice a Christianity that

---

represent 93.1 percent of all daters. This means that only 6.9 percent of all White Christians are willing to date outside of their faith but there are adherents of some faiths that they will not date. Similarly, 93.2 percent of White Christians who attend church at least monthly and 90.2 percent of those that attend church weekly either will date members of all religions or will only date Christians. Among Christians of color, 85.9 percent of all Christians, 85.9 percent of Christians who attend church monthly, and 82.1 percent of Christians who attend church weekly either date only Christians or will date members of all religions.

buttresses their higher racial position (Emerson & Smith, 2000). Such a belief would explain the reluctance of White Christians to jeopardize their current racial standing. Future research should explore whether White Christians are more willing to accept a racialized hierarchy than other Whites and how they may interpret their Christian faith to support such a belief.

References

Aldridge, D. P. (1978). Interracial Marriages: Empirical and Theoretical Considerations. *Journal of Black Studies, 8,* 355–368.

Allport, G. W. (1966). The Religious Context of Prejudice. *Journal for the Scientific Study of Religion, Fall,* 447–457.

Batson, C. D., Schoenrade, P., & Ventis, W. L. (1993). *Religion and the Individual: A Social-Psychological Perspective.* New York: Oxford University Press.

Bonilla-Silva, E. (2001). *White Supremacy and Racism in the Post-Civil Rights Era.* Boulder, CO: Lynne Rienner Publishers.

Bonilla-Silva, E. (2003). *Racism without Racist: Color-Blind Racism and the Persistence of Racial Inequality in the United States.* New York: Rowman and Littlefield.

Buswell, J. O. (1964). *Slavery, Segregation, and Scripture.* Grand Rapids, MI: Eerdmans.

Campos, L. D. S., Otta, E., & Siqueira, J. D. O. (2002). Sex Differences in Mate Selection Strategies: Content Analyses and Responses to Personal Advertisements in Brazil. *Evolution and Human Behavior, 23*(5), 395–406.

Carr, L. G. (1997). *Color-Blind Racism.* Thousand Oaks, CA: Sage Publications.

Chaves, M. (1999). *National Congregational Study.* Tucson, AZ: Department of Sociology, University of Arizona.

Clark, J. (2000). *I Gave Dating a Chance: A Biblical Perspective to Balance the Extremes.* Colorado Springs, CO: Waterbrook Press.

Cloud, H., & Townsend, J. (2000). *Boundaries in Dating*. Grand Rapids, MI: Zondervan.

Daniels, J. (1997). *White Lies: Race, Class, Gender, and Sexuality in White Supremacist Discourse*. New York: Routledge.

Davidson, J. D., & Wilman, T. (2002). The Effect of Group Size on Interfaith Marriage among Catholics. *Journal for the Scientific Study of Religion, 41*(3), 397–404.

Dobson, J. C. (1995, February). Seven Keys to Lifelong Love. *Focus on the Family Magazine, 8.*

Dyer, R. (2002). The Matter of Whiteness. In R. P. S. (Ed.), *White Privilege: Essential Readings on the Other Side of Racism*. New York: Worth.

Emerson, M. O., & Sikkink, D. (Forthcoming). School Choice and Racial Residential Segregation in U.S. Schools: The Role of Parent's Education. *Ethnic and Racial Studies.*

Emerson, M. O., & Smith, C. (2000). *Divided by Faith: Evangelical Religion and the Problem of Race in America*. Oxford: Oxford University Press.

Fang, C. Y., Sidanius, J., & Pratto, F. (1998). Romance across the Social Status Continuum: Interracial Marriage and the Ideological Asymmetry Effect. *Journal of Cross-Cultural Psychology, 29*(2), 290–305.

Feagin, J. R. (2000). *Racist America: Roots, Current Realities, and Future Reparations*. New York: Routledge.

Frame, M. W. (2004). The Challenges of Intercultural Marriage: Strategies for Pastoral Care. *Pastoral Psychology, 52*(3), 219–232.

Frazier, S. T. (2002). *Check All That Apply Finding Wholeness as a Multiracial Person*. Downer Grove, IL: InterVarsity Press.

Gordon, A. I. (1964). *Intermarriage: Interfaith, Interracial, Interethnic*. Boston, MA: Beacon Press.

Hacker, A. (1995). *Two Nations: Black and White, Separate, Hostile, and Unequal*. New York: Ballantine.

Ham, K., Wieland, C., & Batten, D. (2000). *One Blood: The Biblical Answer to Racism*. Green Forest, AR: Master Books Inc.

Jackson, L. M., & Hunsberger, B. (1999). An Intergroup Perspective on Religion and Prejudice. *Journal for the Scientific Study of Religion, September,* 509–523.

Jordan, W. D. (1968). *White over Black.* Baltimore, MD: Penguin.

Kaufman, G., & Phua, V. C. (2003). Is Ageism Alive in Date Selection among Men? Age Requests among Gay and Straight Men in Internet Personal Ads. *Journal of Men's Studies, 11*(2), 225–235.

Keener, C. S. (2002). The Bible and Interracial Marriage. In G. Yancey & S. Yancey (Eds.), *Just Don't Marry One* (pp. 2–27). Valley Forge, PA: Judson Press.

Kirkpatrick, L. A. (1993). Fundamentalism, Christian Orthodoxy, and Intrinsic Religious Orientation as Predictors of Discriminatory Attitudes. *Journal for the Scientific Study of Religion, March,* 256–268.

Knox, D., Zusman, M. E., Buffington, C., & Hemphill, G. (2000). Interracial Dating Attitudes Among College Students. *College Student Journal, 34*(1), 69–76.

Lewis, R., & Yancey, G. (1995). Bi-Racial Marriages in the United States: An Analysis of Variation in Family Member Support of the Decision to Marry. *Sociological Spectrum, 15*(4), 443–462.

Luehrmann, S. (2004). Mediated Marriage: Internet Matchmaking in Provincial Russia. *Europe-Asia Studies, 56*(6), 857–875.

Lynn, M. W., & Bolig, R. (1985). Personal Advertisements: Sources of Data about Relationships. *Journal of Social and Personal Relationships, 2,* 377–383.

McIntosh, P. (2002). White Privilege: Unpacking the Invisible Knapsack. In P. S. Rothenberg (Ed.), *White Privilege: Essential Readings on the Other Side of Racism* (pp. 97–102). New York: Worth.

Montini, T., & Ovrebro, B. (1990). Personal Relationship Ads: An Informal Balancing Act. *Sociological Perspectives, 33*(3), 327–339.

Myra, H. (1994). Love in Black and White. *Christianity Today, 38,* 18–19.

Oliver, M. L., & Shapiro, T. M. (1995). *Black Wealth/White Wealth: A New Perspective on Racial Inequality.* New York: Russell Sage Foundation.

Pawlowski, B., & Koziel, S. (2002). The Impact of Traits Offered in Personal Advertisements on Response Rates. *Evolution and Human Behavior, 23*(2), 139–149.

Phillips, R. D., & Phillips, S. L. (2006). *Holding Hands, Holding Hearts: Recovering a Biblical View of Christian Dating.* Phillipsburg, NJ: P & R Publishing.

Phua, V. C. (2002). Sex and Sexuality in Men's Personal Advertisements. *Men and Masculinities, 5*(2), 178–191.

Phua, V. C., & Kaufman, G. (2003). The Crossroads of Race and Sexuality: Date Selection among Men in Internet "Personal" Ads. *Journal of Family Issues, 24*(8), 981–994.

Rice, M., & Rice, V. (1981). *When Can I Say I Love You.* Chicago, IL: Moody Press.

Roberts, K. A. (2003). *Religion in the Sociological Perspective* (4th ed.). Belmont, CA: Wadsworth.

Romano, R. (2003). *Race Mixing: Black-White Marriage in Postwar America.* Cambridge, MA: Harvard University Press.

Sautter, J., Tippett, B., & Morgan, S. P. (2006). *Check out my Profile: Demographic Characteristics of the Internet Dating Population.* Paper presented at the Southern Sociological Society Meetings, New Orleans, LA.

Sears, D. O. (1988). Symbolic Racism. In P. A. Katz & D. A. Taylor (Eds.), *Eliminating Racism: Profiles in Controversy* (pp. 53–84). New York: Plenum Press.

Silverstein, A. (2001). Modernists vs. Traditionalists: Competition and Legitimacy within American Conservative Judaism. In E. Lederhendler (Ed.), *Who Owns Judaism?: Public Religion and Private Faith in America and Israel.* New York: Oxford University Press.

Smith, J. E., Waldorf, V. A., & Trembath, D. L. (1990). Single White Male Looking for Thin, Very Attractive … *Sex Roles, 23*, 675–685.

Sniderman, P., & Tetlock, P. E. (1986). Symbolic Racism: Problems of Motive Attribution in Political Analysis. *Journal of Social Issues, 42*, 129–150.

Spickard, P. (1989). *Mixed Blood: Intermarriage and Ethnic Identity in Twentieth-century America*. Thousand Oaks, CA: Sage.

Stember, C. H. (1976). *Sexual Racism*. New York: Harper and Row.

Toro-Morn, M., & Sprecher, S. (2003). A Cross-Cultural Comparison of Mate Preferences among University Students; The United States vs. The People's Republic of China. *Journal of Comparative Family Studies, 34*(2), 151–170.

Twine, F. W. (1997). Brown-Skinned White Girls: Class, Culture, and the Construction of White Identity in Suburban Communities. In R. Frankenberg (Ed.), *Displacing Whiteness: Essays in Social and Cultural Criticism*. Durham, NC: Duke University Press.

University, B. (2005). *The Baylor Religion Survey*. Waco, TX: Baylor Institute for Studies of Religion.

Van Ausdale, D., & Feagin, J. R. (2001). *The First R: How Children Learn Race and Racism*. Lanham, MD: Rowman and Littlefield.

Van Der Post, L. (1955). *The Dark Eye in Africa*. New York: Morrow.

Wilmore, G. S. (1972). *Black Religion and Black Radicalism*. Garden City, NY: Doubleday.

Yancey, G. (2003). *Who is White?: Latinos, Asians, and the New Black/Nonblack Divide*. Boulder, CO: Lynne Rienner.

Yancey, G. (Unpublished paper). Who we will Date: Using Internet Personal Advertisements to Examine Endogamy.

Yancey, G., & Yancey, S. (1997). Black-White Differences in the Use of Personal Advertisements for Individuals Seeking Interracial Relationships. *Journal of Black Studies, 27*(5), 650–667.

Yancey, G., & Yancey, S. (1998). Interracial Dating: Evidence from the Personal Advertisements. *Journal of Family Issues, 19*(3), 334–348.

Chapter 8

Conclusion: Where Do Interracial Relationships Go from Here?

Angela Hattery & Earl Smith

The essays in this book, *Interracial Relationships in the 21st Century,* have covered a wide range of topics at the core of both scholarly research and public discourse and debates about interracial relationships in the 21st century United States. In this text, we have brought together some of the leading scholars who have published in the area of interracial relationships and their essays provide fuel for intellectual debates as well as suggestions for the future.

Where do we go from here? As we enter the 21st Century in the United States we enter a period in which more and more people are entering unions that cross racial/ethnic boundaries and more and more individuals identify themselves using some multiracial/multi-ethnic label. As noted in the introduction, at the time of the writing of this book, Barack Obama has become the first African American president of the United States. Of course, the issues raised in this book, and by Mr. Obama himself, point to the ever-changing definitions of race. Is Mr. Obama "African American" or is he "biracial" or is he of "African descent" or is his racial identity simply a matter of his own articulation, much the same way that Tiger Woods claims "Cablinasian."[1]

Does it matter?

---

1. There is a lot of discussion about Woods and his choice of this term, one he coined from Caucasian, Black, (American) Indian, and Asian—all a part of his parental heritage. A good discussion of this is found in Smith,

Yes. But only because the changing landscape allows for individuals to claim identities that make sense to them. In the long history of the United States, this has never happened before. Individuals who have parents of different races/ethnicities are no longer forced to preference one ancestry or community over another. Though, as Rockquemore and Laszloffy point out in Chapter Four, this is not without consequences.

Racial identity and the changing racial landscape also matter because identities can be used to downplay power. If Mr. Obama is viewed by White Americans as "biracial" does that minimize the fact that he is also "Black?" Does this make him less threatening as a potential contender for the most powerful position in the global political economy? Or are barriers set up to deny access to the opportunity structure based on Whites' notions of race—which is constructed primarily around skin color—regardless of an individual's own racial identity? The fact that Tiger Woods identifies as "cablinasian" doesn't prevent announcers from referring to him as the first "African American" golfer to win the Masters nor does it prevent country clubs in San Diego, or Birmingham from denying him a membership because they do not allow African Americas to become members.

In other words, race and racial identity continue to matter at both the personal and structural level. And, whereas many people feel freer now to self-identify using the new multi-racial/multi-ethnic lexicon this only masks or distracts us from the fact that structural racism continues to dominate every aspect of the U.S. social political economy.

In this context, a book like this is designed to raise more questions than it answers, to illustrate the complexities and challenges of crossing racial barriers. Secondly, this book moves us beyond simple categories of "Black" and "White." For example, in her chapter, Wei Ming explores the co-opting of the term Hapa from individuals of Hawaiian descent by a variety of Asian Americans with roots in many different nation-states.

Earl. 2007. *Race, Sport and the American Dream*. Durham, North Carolina: Carolina Academic Press.

This book also moves us beyond a simplistic discussions of race as an isolated social status and forces us to grapple with the ways that race intersects with other identities such as sexuality and spirituality.

This book forces us to think about the contours of race, identity, intimacy, and family as it occurs in the contemporary United States. And, if further trends in interracial coupling continue, we can predict that the issues raised in these chapters will only become more relevant.

Furthermore, we are entering a period in our history in which, for the first time, "Whites" will comprise less than half of the U.S. population and Hispanics will become the "majority-minority." Whether individuals themselves enter into unions and create families that cross racial/ethnic lines, our culture will continue to be challenged to absorb an even more diverse population, to grapple with shifting and competing demands, and to address issues of power and oppression as they are constructed along racial/ethnic lines. These issues will not be easy to deal with, they will create antagonism and change will not come easily. We conclude this book by asking what role individual relationships that cross the policed-boundaries of race/ethnicity will play in opening up institutional power structures that have historically been built on a race line defined in its most simple terms: White and non-White. What role will multi-racial individuals, families and communities play in stretching our constructions of race? What role might a biracial president play in expanding our national conversation on race? Will it be similar or different to the contributions of public figures of the past—from Thomas Jefferson to Clarence Thomas—who have grappled with crossing racial boundaries in their own families while being charged with maintaining racial boundaries as a matter of law? Where we go from here will be determined by both individual experiences with the "color line" and the ability—or not—of institutions and social structures to open up access to an increasingly diverse, increasingly complex population.

References

Smith, Earl. 2007. *Race, Sport and the American Dream*. Durham, North Carolina: Carolina Academic Press.

Index